HAMPTON-BROWN
HIGH POINT
SUCCESS IN LANGUAGE • LITERATURE • CONTENT

Language Practice Book
The Basics

HAMPTON-BROWN

Hampton-Brown
P.O. Box 223220
Carmel, California 93922
1-800-333-3510

Printed in the United States of America
ISBN 0-7362-1231-0

08 09 10 11 16 15 14

Contents: Language Practice Book for Lakeside School

© Hampton-Brown

Language Practice Book Contents

© Hampton-Brown

Lakeside School

85 LAKE AVENUE

Numbers and Number Words

Say each number. Read each number word.

1 one	**21** twenty-one	**110** one hundred ten
2 two	**22** twenty-two	**120** one hundred twenty
3 three	**23** twenty-three	**130** one hundred thirty
4 four	**24** twenty-four	**140** one hundred forty
5 five	**25** twenty-five	**150** one hundred fifty
6 six	**26** twenty-six	**160** one hundred sixty
7 seven	**27** twenty-seven	**170** one hundred seventy
8 eight	**28** twenty-eight	**180** one hundred eighty
9 nine	**29** twenty-nine	**190** one hundred ninety
10 ten	**30** thirty	**200** two hundred
11 eleven	**40** forty	
12 twelve	**50** fifty	
13 thirteen	**60** sixty	
14 fourteen	**70** seventy	
15 fifteen	**80** eighty	
16 sixteen	**90** ninety	
17 seventeen	**100** one hundred	
18 eighteen	**101** one hundred one	
19 nineteen		
20 twenty		

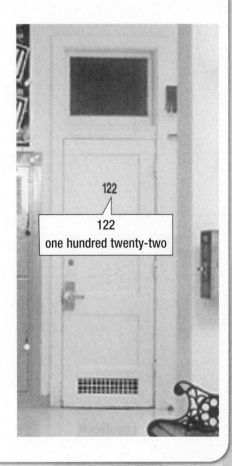

122

122
one hundred twenty-two

Numbers and Number Words

Look at each picture. Find the number. Say it.
Then write the number word.

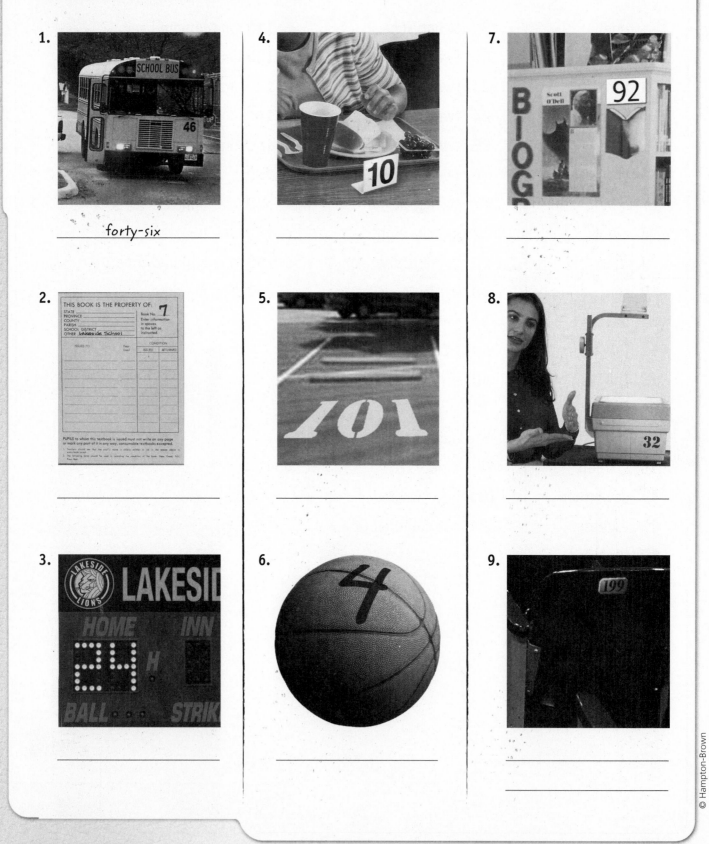

1. _forty-six_

2. _____

3. _____

4. _____

5. _____

6. _____

7. _____

8. _____

9. _____

© Hampton-Brown

School Locations

Draw the main building of your school. Use these words to add the names of things. Add the names of other things you know.

window   fence   steps
door   bench   sidewalk

This is _____ .

Give Information

What are these things? Write their names.
Put a ✓ next to the ones you find in
your school.

bench	door	gym	street
bulletin board	fence	light	truck
clock	flag	room number	van
crosswalk	garbage can	school bus	window

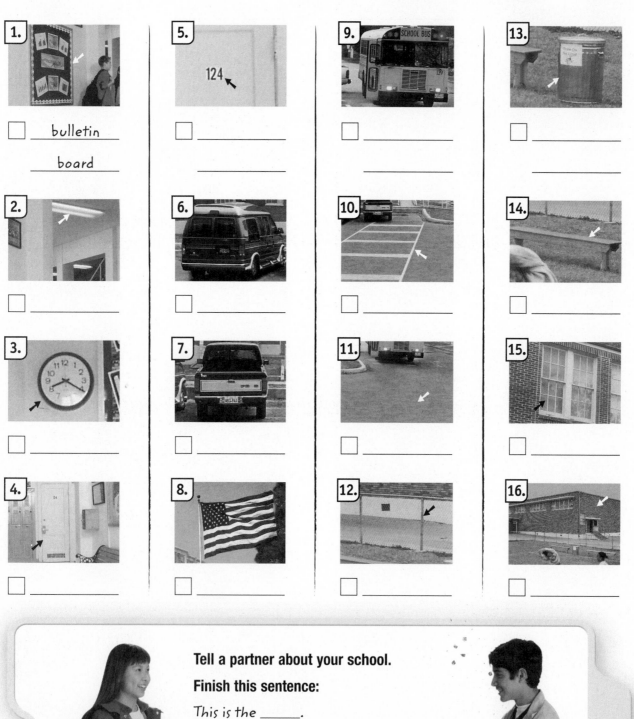

1. ☐ bulletin board

2. ☐ _____

3. ☐ _____

4. ☐ _____

5. ☐ _____

6. ☐ _____

7. ☐ _____

8. ☐ _____

9. ☐ _____

10. ☐ _____

11. ☐ _____

12. ☐ _____

13. ☐ _____

14. ☐ _____

15. ☐ _____

16. ☐ _____

Tell a partner about your school.

Finish this sentence:

This is the _____.

Make as many sentences as you can.

© Hampton-Brown

Classroom Objects

Look at each picture. Write the words to complete the sentence.

board	desk	notebook	ruler
book	eraser	pen	stapler
bookcase	highlighter	pencil	window

1.

Here is a ___book___ .

2.

Here is _____

_____ .

3.

Here _____

_____ .

4.

_____

_____ .

5.

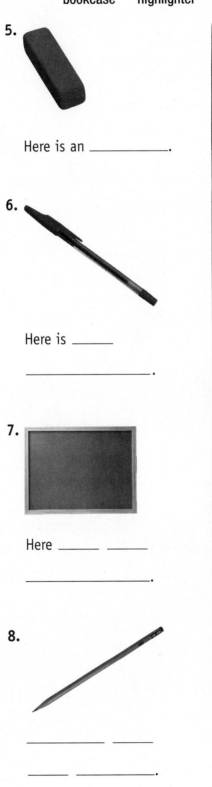

Here is an _____ .

6.

Here is _____

_____ .

7.

Here _____ _____

_____ .

8.

_____

_____ .

9.

Here is a _____ .

10.

Here is _____

_____ .

11.

Here _____ _____

_____ .

12.

_____

_____ .

Ask and Answer Questions

How to Play

1. **Play with a partner.**

2. **Make a spinner. Put it in the circle.**

3. **Partner 1 spins and asks a question.**

   Examples: Is this a pencil? Is this an eraser?

4. **Partner 2 answers.**

   Examples: Yes. This is a pencil. No. This is a book.

5. **Then Partner 2 spins.**

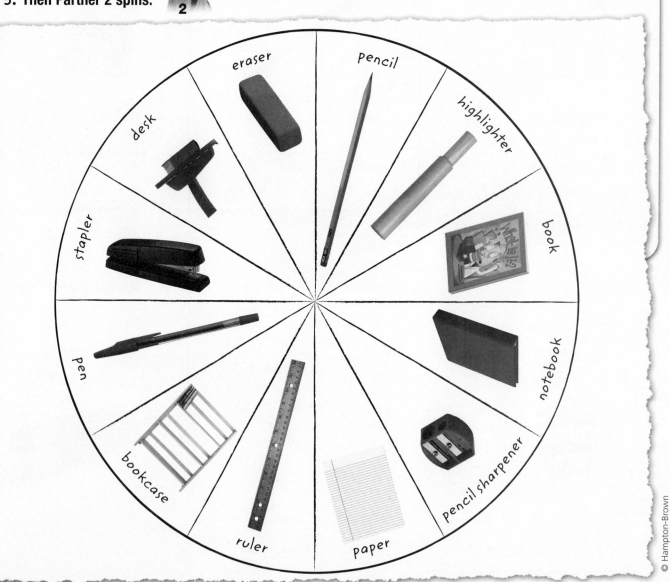

© Hampton-Brown

Greetings

Read the speech balloons below. What does Maylin say first? Write the words in the first speech balloon. Then complete the other speech balloons.

Hi.

Hello, Mrs. Terry. This is Carlos.

Welcome, Carlos. Nice to meet you.

Carlos, this is Mrs. Terry.

1.

2.

3.

4.

Now act out the scene with two partners.

School Locations

Put a ✓ next to each place in your school.
Add the names of other places in your school.

✓ girls' bathroom	☐ main office	☐ cafeteria	☐ _____
☐ boys' bathroom	☐ entrance	☐ auditorium	☐ _____
☐ library	☐ gym	☐ counselor's office	☐ _____

Draw a map of your school. Then write the names on your map.

This is _____ .

Ask Questions

How to Play

1. Play with a partner.

2. Use the school map in *Lakeside School*.

3. Use an eraser or other small object as your game piece.
   Use a coin to show how many spaces to move.

  Heads = 1 space    Tails = 2 spaces

4. Read the question. Point to the answer on the school map.

5. The first one to reach FINISH wins.

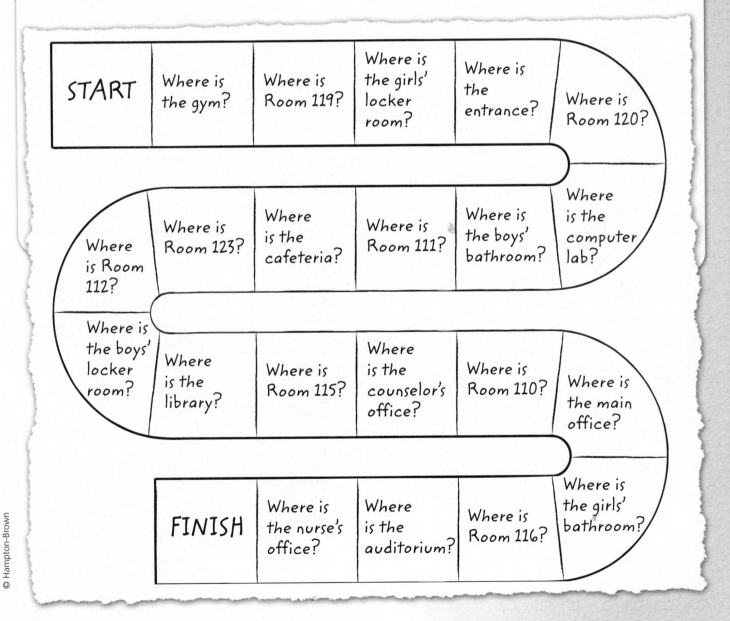

| START | Where is the gym? | Where is Room 119? | Where is the girls' locker room? | Where is the entrance? | Where is Room 120? |

Where is Room 112?

Where is Room 123?

Where is the cafeteria?

Where is Room 111?

Where is the boys' bathroom?

Where is the computer lab?

Where is the boys' locker room?

Where is the library?

Where is Room 115?

Where is the counselor's office?

Where is Room 110?

Where is the main office?

FINISH

Where is the nurse's office?

Where is the auditorium?

Where is Room 116?

Where is the girls' bathroom?

Telling Time

Read the time on each clock.

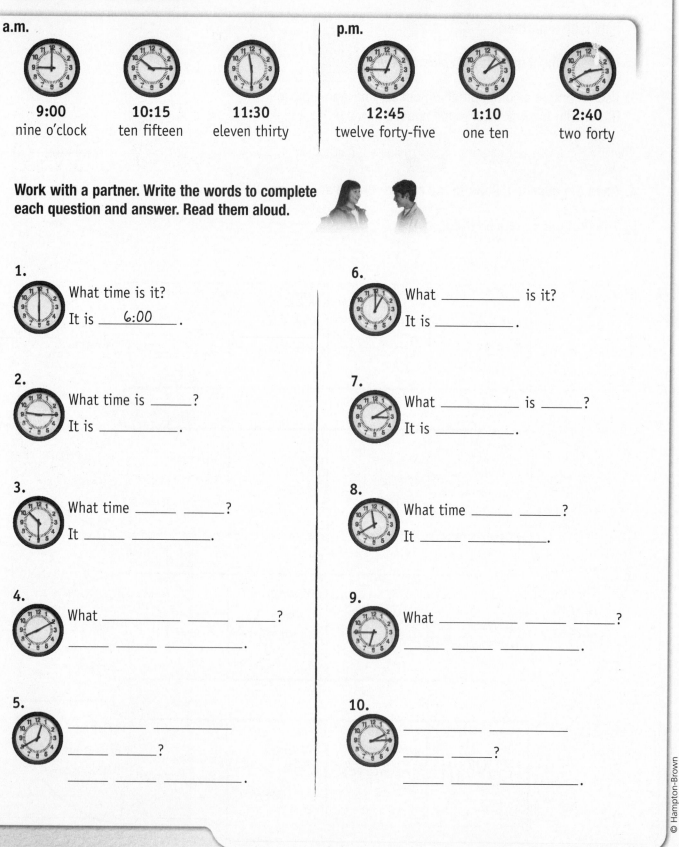

a.m.

9:00
nine o'clock

10:15
ten fifteen

11:30
eleven thirty

p.m.

12:45
twelve forty-five

1:10
one ten

2:40
two forty

Work with a partner. Write the words to complete each question and answer. Read them aloud.

1.
What time is it?
It is ___6:00___ .

2.
What time is _____?
It is _____ .

3.
What time _____ _____?
It _____ _____ .

4.
What _____ _____?
_____ _____ _____ .

5.
_____ _____
_____ _____?
_____ _____ .

6.
What _____ is it?
It is _____ .

7.
What _____ is _____?
It is _____ .

8.
What time _____ _____?
It _____ _____ .

9.
What _____ _____ _____?
_____ _____ _____ .

10.
_____ _____
_____ _____?
_____ _____ .

Ask and Answer Questions

Write your class schedule in this chart.

ESL	Math	Science
Homeroom	P.E.	Social Studies
Language Arts	Reading	Lunch

_____ 's Class Schedule

Class	Time	Room	Teacher

Work with a partner. Ask about his or her schedule. Answer your partner's questions.

Examples: Where is your math class? It's in Room 124.
Who is your teacher? Mr. Rosario.

Give Information

Look at each picture. Write *Here is* or *Here are* to complete each sentence.

1.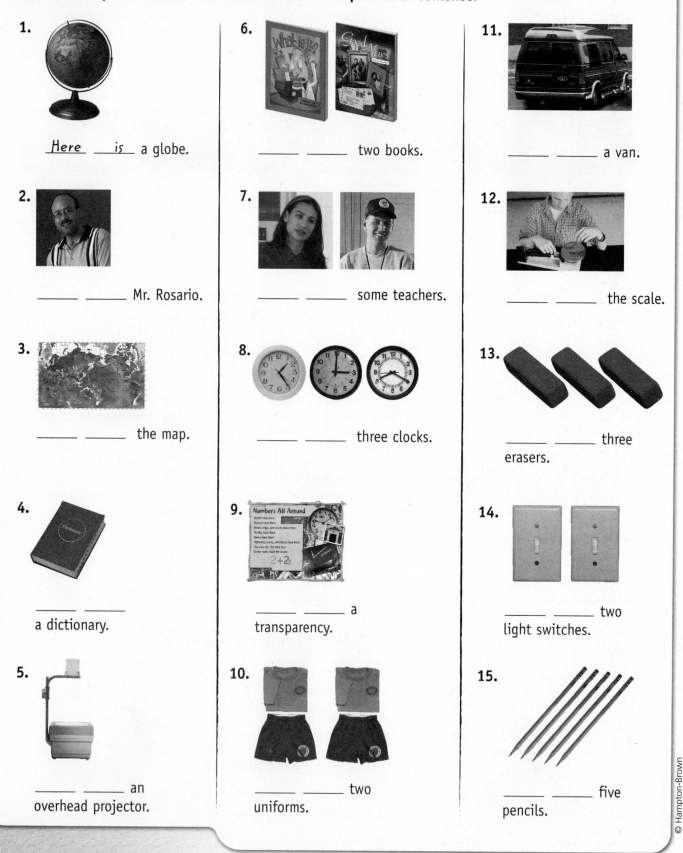

   <u>Here</u> <u>is</u> a globe.

2. _____ _____ Mr. Rosario.

3. _____ _____ the map.

4. _____ _____ a dictionary.

5. _____ _____ an overhead projector.

6. _____ _____ two books.

7. _____ _____ some teachers.

8. _____ _____ three clocks.

9. _____ _____ a transparency.

10. _____ _____ two uniforms.

11. _____ _____ a van.

12. _____ _____ the scale.

13. _____ _____ three erasers.

14. _____ _____ two light switches.

15. _____ _____ five pencils.

© Hampton-Brown

Classroom Activities

Look at each picture. Write the word to complete each sentence.

point   read   work

raise   show   write

1.

I ____work____ at my desk.

2.

I _____ my hand.

3.

I _____ a problem on the board.

4.

I _____ the answer to the problem.

I _____ my work.

5.

I _____ to the correct answer.

6.

I _____ my textbook.

7.

I _____ my name on my worksheet.

8.

I _____ my worksheet.

I _____ the answers.

Shapes

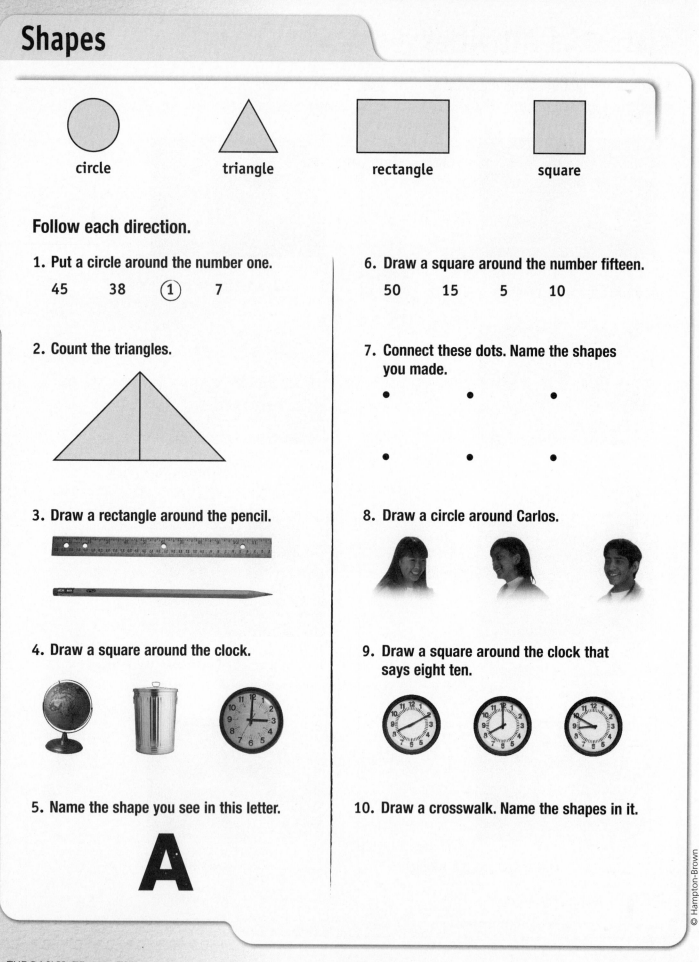

circle   triangle   rectangle   square

Follow each direction.

1. **Put a circle around the number one.**

   45   38   ①   7

2. **Count the triangles.**

3. **Draw a rectangle around the pencil.**

4. **Draw a square around the clock.**

5. **Name the shape you see in this letter.**

   A

6. **Draw a square around the number fifteen.**

   50   15   5   10

7. **Connect these dots. Name the shapes you made.**

8. **Draw a circle around Carlos.**

9. **Draw a square around the clock that says eight ten.**

10. **Draw a crosswalk. Name the shapes in it.**

Give and Carry Out Commands

How to Play

1. Play with a partner.

2. Use an eraser or other small object as your game piece.
   Use a coin to show how many spaces to move.

   Heads = 1 space   Tails = 2 spaces

3. Read the command in the space. Then do it.

4. The first one to reach FINISH wins.

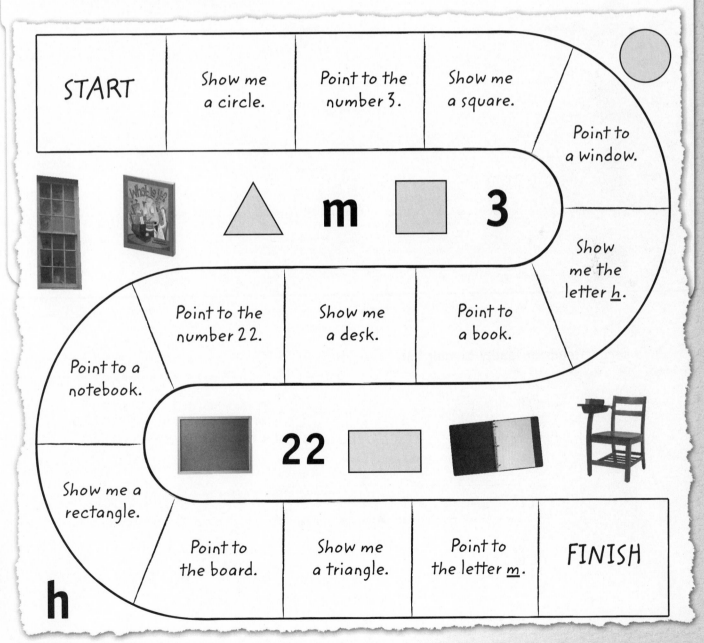

| START | Show me a circle. | Point to the number 3. | Show me a square. |

Point to a window.

Show me the letter _h_.

Point to the number 22. | Show me a desk. | Point to a book.

Point to a notebook.

Show me a rectangle.

Point to the board. | Show me a triangle. | Point to the letter _m_. | FINISH

Personal Information

Look at the names and phone numbers. Complete each sentence.

Carlos
555-6937

Maylin
555-9731

Lupe
555-9664

Ron
555-2544

Imran
555-0056

1. My name is __*Carlos*__. My phone number is ____555-6937____.

2. My name _____ _____. My phone number _____ _____.

3. My _____ _____ _____. My phone number _____ _____.

4. _____ name _____ _____.
   My _____ _____ _____ _____.

5. _____ _____ _____ _____.
   _____ _____ _____ _____.

Add some friends or family to your list.

6. ☐ My name is _____.
   My phone number is _____.

7. ☐ _____ _____ _____.
   _____ _____ _____ _____.

8. ☐ _____ _____ _____.
   _____ _____ _____ _____.

Ask for Information

Read each question to a partner. Write the answers to the questions your partner reads.

Ask:	Your Answer:
1. What is your name?	
2. Where is your school?	
3. What is the name of your school?	
4. Where is your English class?	
5. What is the room number for your science class?	
6. What is in your science classroom?	
7. Where is your social studies class?	
8. What is the room number for your homeroom?	
9. Where is a bench?	
10. Where is a flag?	

Express Needs

Look at each picture. Complete the sentence. Tell what you need to do.

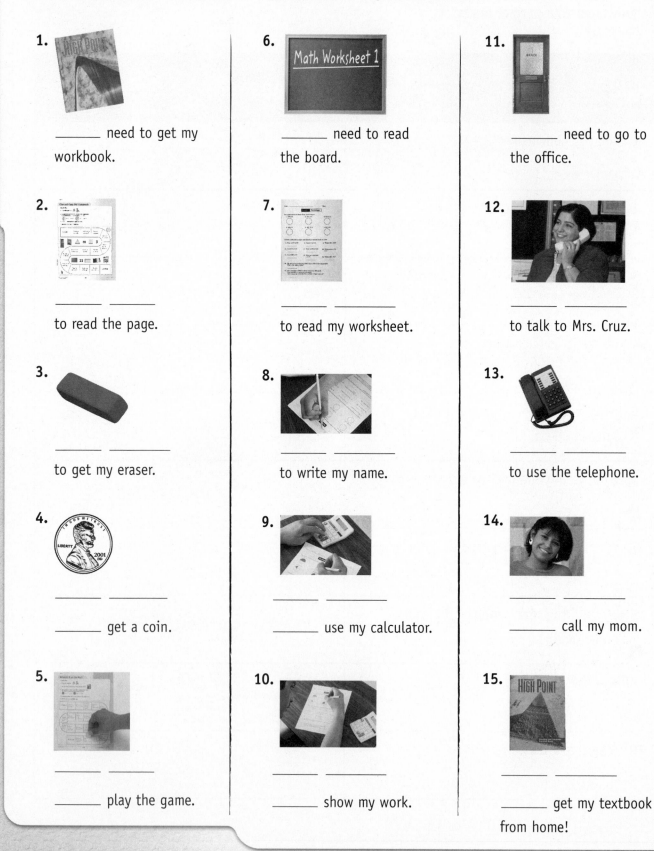

1. _____ need to get my workbook.

2. _____ to read the page.

3. _____ to get my eraser.

4. _____ get a coin.

5. _____ play the game.

6. _____ need to read the board.

7. _____ to read my worksheet.

8. _____ to write my name.

9. _____ use my calculator.

10. _____ show my work.

11. _____ need to go to the office.

12. _____ to talk to Mrs. Cruz.

13. _____ to use the telephone.

14. _____ call my mom.

15. _____ get my textbook from home!

Name _____

Ask for and Give Information

Put a ✓ next to each thing that is in your library. Add the names of more things.

- ✓ bookcase
- ☐ magazine
- ☐ book
- ☐ table
- ☐ chair
- ☐ cart
- ☐ globe
- ☐ computer
- ☐ printer
- ☐ newspaper
- ☐ encyclopedia
- ☐ book return box
- ☐ _____
- ☐ _____
- ☐ _____

Work with a partner. Make each word above plural.

Example: bookcase—bookcases

Look at each picture. Write the words to complete the sentence.

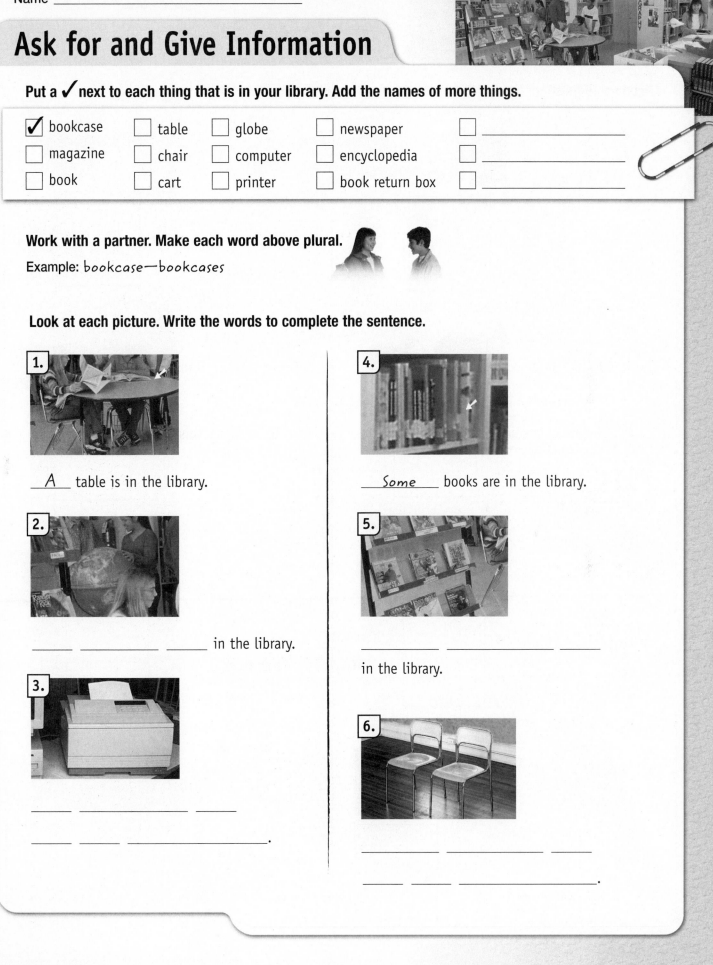

1.

___A___ table is in the library.

2.

_____ _____ _____ in the library.

3.

_____ _____ _____
_____ _____ _____ .

4.

___Some___ books are in the library.

5.

_____ _____ _____
in the library.

6.

_____ _____ _____
_____ _____ _____ .

© Hampton-Brown

Tell What You Like

Read each question. Answer it. Then draw a picture of your answer.

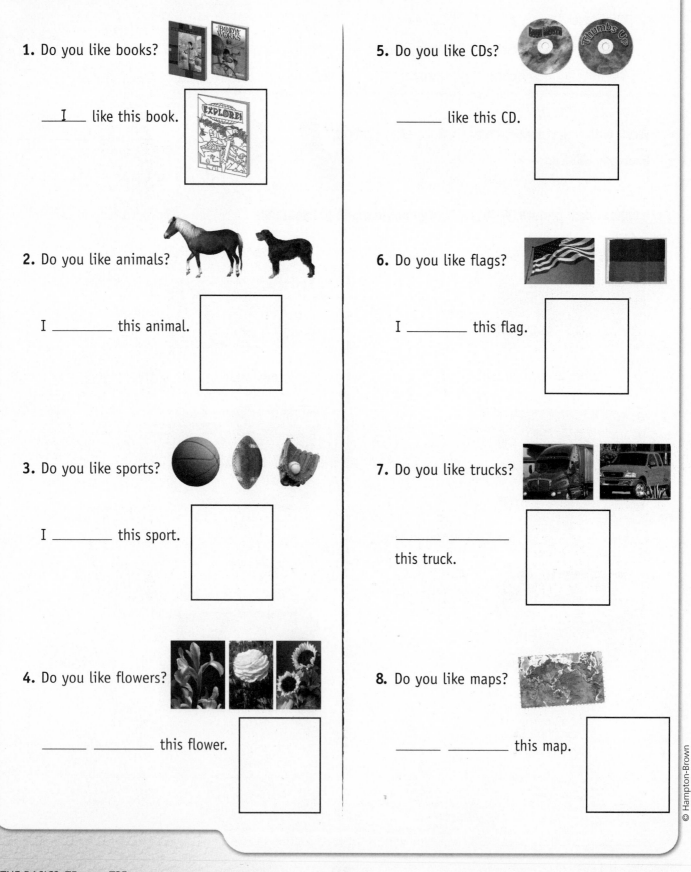

1. Do you like books?

___I___ like this book.

2. Do you like animals?

I _____ this animal.

3. Do you like sports?

I _____ this sport.

4. Do you like flowers?

_____ _____ this flower.

5. Do you like CDs?

_____ like this CD.

6. Do you like flags?

I _____ this flag.

7. Do you like trucks?

_____ _____ this truck.

8. Do you like maps?

_____ _____ this map.

© Hampton-Brown

Ask and Answer Questions

Write *Does* or *Will you* to complete each question.

1. _Will you_ help me find a book?

Yes, I will.

_____ the book show a picture of soccer?

No. It shows other sports.

2. _____ your mom work at a school?

No. She works at the bank.

_____ show me where the cafeteria is?

Yes. Come with me.

3. _____ help me call my mom?

Yes, I will!

_____ please tell me the phone number of the school?

Yes. It's 555-1000.

4. _____ my group need to draw pictures?

No. Please use the tiles.

_____ give me the tiles?

Yes. Here they are.

Tell What You Like

Put a ✓ next to the sports you like. Add the names of other sports.

☐ basketball   ☐ volleyball   ☐ _____

☐ softball   ☐ soccer   ☐ _____

☐ track   ☐ _____

Now draw some sports you like. Complete each sentence.

1.

_I_ _like_ _____.

2.

___ ___ _____.

3.

___ ___ _____.

4.

___ ___ _____.

They Don't Feel Well!

Write the words to complete each sentence.   He   She   They   have   has

1.

_____She_____ has a headache.

2.

They _____ fevers.

3.

_____ has a toothache.

4.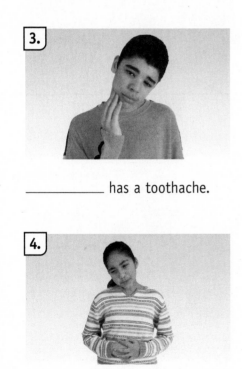

She _____ a stomachache.

5.

He _____ a cold.

6.

_____ have stomachaches.

7.

He _____ a fever.

8.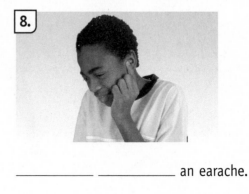

_____ _____ an earache.

Express Feelings

How to Play

1. **Play with a partner.**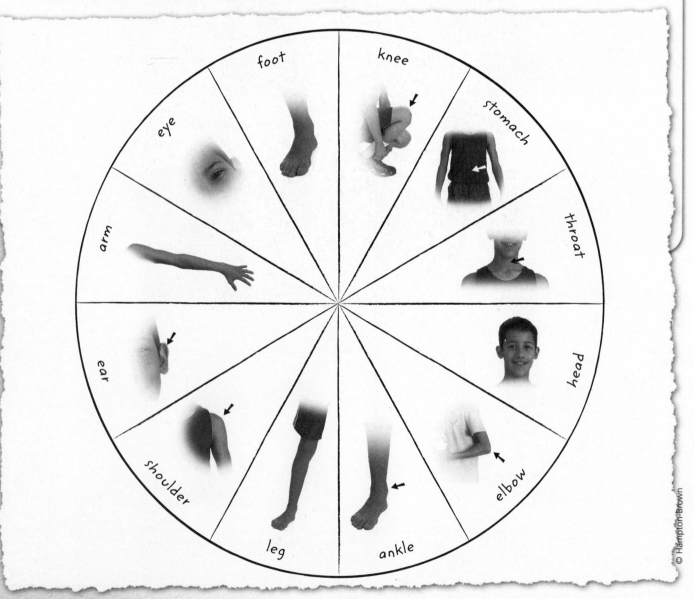

2. **Make a spinner. Put it in the circle.**

3. **Partner 1 spins and acts like that body part hurts.** Partner 2 asks: *How do you feel?*

4. **Partner 1 answers.** Examples: My leg hurts. My arm hurts.

5. **Then Partner 2 spins.**

6. **The person who names all 12 body parts first wins.**

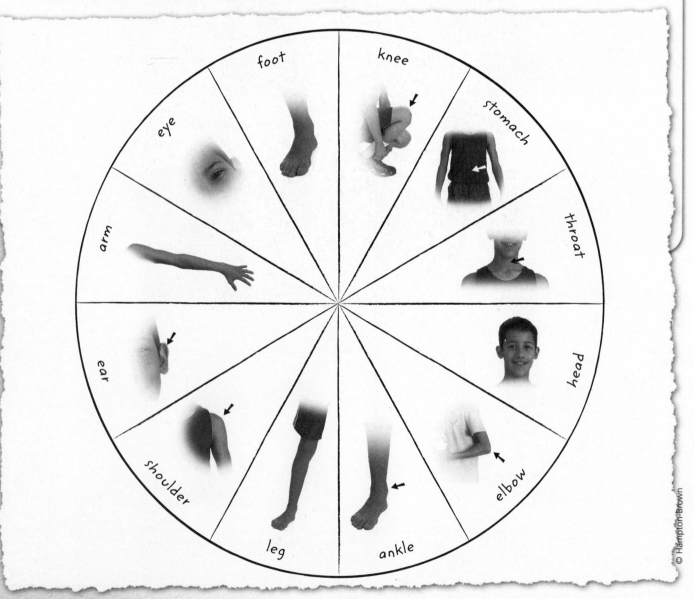

© Hampton-Brown

Ask and Answer Questions

Write the words to complete each question and answer.

bad	fine	How	do	feels
better	sick	feel	does	

1.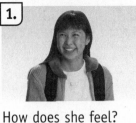

How does she feel?

She ___*feels*___ fine.

2.

How do they _____?

_____ feel _____.

3.

How does she _____?

_____ _____ _____.

4.

_____ does he feel?

_____ _____ _____.

5.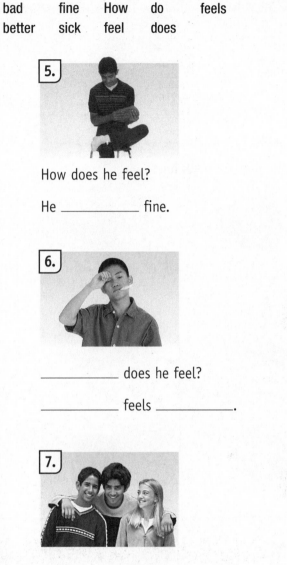

How does he feel?

He _____ fine.

6.

_____ does he feel?

_____ feels _____.

7.

_____ do they _____?

_____ _____ _____.

8.

_____ does _____ _____?

_____ _____ _____.

Name _____

Food

Put a ✓ next to each food you like. Add other foods you like.

☐ apple   ☐ egg   ☐ salad   ☐ _____

☐ applesauce   ☐ hamburger   ☐ sandwich   ☐ _____

☐ bagel   ☐ hot dog   ☐ soup   ☐ _____

☐ cake   ☐ pizza   ☐ taco and beans   ☐ _____

Write the name of each food.

1. taco and beans

2. _____

3. _____

4. _____

5. _____

6. _____

7. _____

8. _____

9. _____

10. _____

11. _____

12. _____

Draw a picture of a food you like and a picture of a food you do not like. Tell a partner about them.

I like _____.

I do not like _____.

Money

What can you buy for $2.00?

25¢	**30¢**	**$1.00**	**50¢**	**$1.00**
$1.00	**$1.25**	**15¢**	**90¢**	**75¢**
50¢	**80¢**	**60¢**	**$1.20**	**90¢**

Foods

What would you like to eat for lunch?

sandwich	egg	soup	apple	milk
cottage cheese	salad	cookie	taco and beans	hamburger
hot dog	macaroni and cheese	bagel	pizza	cake

Science Materials and Activities

**Put a ✓ next to each science material that is in your science lab.
Add other materials you see there.**

☐ model	☐ notes	☐ scale
☐ cabinet	☐ poster	☐ _____
☐ microscope	☐ ruler	☐ _____

Look at each picture. Write the word to complete the sentence.

1.

I _____listen_____ to the teacher.
listen   observe

2.

I _____ trays.
get   listen

3.

I _____ an experiment.
measure   do

4.

I _____.
take   measure

5.

I _____.
observe   take

6.

I _____ notes.
listen   take

Needs and Thoughts

Write *I need* or *I think* to complete each sentence.

1. I need some ice for my ankle.

2. _____ P.E. is fun.

3. _____ your homework.

4. _____ to give you this note.

5. _____ you have a good schedule.

6. _____ to pay for my food.

7. _____ you can learn this poem.

8. _____ to use a calculator.

9. _____ I know the answer.

10. _____ two tiles.

11. _____ to call my mom.

12. _____ you will like this book.

Clothing and Colors

How to Play

1. **Color each piece of clothing.**

2. **Play with a partner.** **Each partner chooses a sign.** X O

3. **Partner 1 says the color and name of a piece of clothing and marks the square with his or her sign.**

4. **Then Partner 2 takes a turn.**

5. **Get 3 X's or O's in a row to win.**

Ask and Answer Questions

Write the words to complete each answer.

I like this   I like these
I like that   I like those

1. Which T-shirt do you like?

   I like this T-shirt.

2. Which shorts do you like?

   _____ _____ shorts.

3. Which pants do you like?

   _____ _____ pants.

4. Which sweatshirt do you like?

   _____ _____ sweatshirt.

5. Which cap do you like?

   _____ _____ cap.

6. Which socks do you like?

   _____ _____ socks.

Days of the Week

Look at the school sign. Write the words to complete each sentence. Read the answers to a partner.

1. There is a big dance

   on _____.

2. Back-to-School Night is

   on _____.

3. There is a football game

   on _____.

4. The soccer team has a car wash

   on _____.

5. The science club meets

   on _____.

6. There is a teacher meeting

   on _____.

7. _____ is the first
   day of school! Welcome back!

LAKESIDE SCHOOL

THE FIRST WEEK AT LAKESIDE:

MONDAY: WELCOME BACK

TUESDAY: TEACHER MEETING

WEDNESDAY: BACK-TO-SCHOOL NIGHT

THURSDAY: SCIENCE CLUB

FRIDAY: WELCOME BACK DANCE

SATURDAY: FOOTBALL GAME

SUNDAY: SOCCER TEAM CAR WASH

Tell a partner about your week.

Finish this sentence:

On _____ , I _____ .

Make as many sentences as you can.

Good-byes

Write different ways to say good-bye.

See you soon!   See you Tuesday!
See you later!   Bye!
Good-bye!   So long!

© Hampton-Brown

Months of the Year

Draw a picture of something you do each month.
Then write a sentence to tell about it.

January	February	March
_____	_____	_____
April	May	June
_____	_____	_____
July	August	September
_____	_____	_____
October	November	December
_____	_____	_____

Action Verbs

**Read each sentence. <u>Underline</u> the word that tells what
Carlos does. Circle the final _s_ in each action word.**

1.

Carlos <u>meets</u> Maylin.

2.

Carlos points to Room 124.

3.

Carlos raises his hand.

4.

Carlos writes on the board.

5.

Carlos shows his work.

6.

Carlos works with a group.

7.

Carlos looks at the food.

8.

Carlos observes the leaf.

9.

Carlos takes notes.

Draw a line to match each picture and the sentence that tells about it.

10. Carlos reads.

11. Carlos plays.

12. Carlos listens.

13. Carlos writes.

Action Verbs

Write a word to complete each sentence.
asks   gives   points
dances   listens   reads

1. Maylin ___listens___ to the teacher.

2. Maylin _____ a note to Mrs. Cruz.

3. Maylin _____ a magazine.

4. Maylin _____ a question.

5. Maylin _____ to Room 124.

6. Maylin _____ .

Draw two pictures. In each picture, show a friend doing something. Write a sentence to tell what your friend does.

© Hampton-Brown

I am fine
How are you

We are fine.
Thank you!

Bye!
Have a nice day!

Good-bye!

Units 1-18

PRONOUNS

Use Pronouns in Greetings

Study the chart.

Greetings and Good-byes

Greetings	Questions and Answers	Good-byes
Hi!	How are you?	Bye!
Hello!	I am fine.	Good-bye!
Good morning!	We are fine, thank you.	So long!
Good afternoon!	How are you today?	Have a nice day!
Nice to meet you!	I am okay.	See you later!
	We are well, thanks.	

Pronouns

Use **I** to talk about yourself.

  I am happy.

Use **you** when you talk to someone else.

  You are nice.

Use **we** to talk about yourself and someone else.

  We are friends.

Write what the people say. Use the chart.

1. Good morning! / Hello!

Greetings

2. How are you? / I am fine. How are you?

Question and Answer

3. We are fine, thank you. / And how are you?

Question and Answer

4. Bye! Have a nice day! / Good-bye! / Good-bye!

Good-byes

PRONOUNS

Who Is It?

When you talk about other people or things, use the correct pronoun.

For a girl or a woman, use *she*.

She is a student.

For a thing, use *it*.

It is a present.

For a boy or a man, use *he*.

He is a student, too.

Use *they* to talk about more than one person or thing.

They are friends.

Complete each sentence. Add the correct pronoun.

1. Josef and Mikka sit together.

   __They__ are friends.

2. Mikka is 13 years old today.

   __She__ is a teenager now.

3. Josef has a present for Mikka.

   __He__ is a good friend.

4. Mikka likes surprises.

   __She__ takes the present.

5. The present makes Mikka smile.

   __It__ is a CD by her favorite band.

6. The friends laugh.

   __They__ are happy.

© Hampton-Brown

PRESENT TENSE VERBS: *AM*, *IS*, AND *ARE*

They Are in a Race

Use the verbs *am*, *is*, and *are* correctly.

Pronoun	Verb	Example
I	am	I **am** in P.E. class.
he she it	is	He **is** slow. She **is** in front of me. It **is** a nice day.
we you they	are	We **are** happy. You **are** fast! They **are** outside.

Complete each sentence. Add the correct verb.

1.

I __am__ Lisa.

2.

She __is__ in this race, too.

3.

He __is__ behind us.

4.

I __am__ not as fast as Jan.

5.

We say, "You __are__ the winner, Jan!"

6.

Now we __are__ ready to rest.

VOCABULARY: COMMUNICATION

How Can You Communicate?

Name each picture. Use words from the box.

| letter | ~~fax~~ | phone | ~~e-mail~~ |

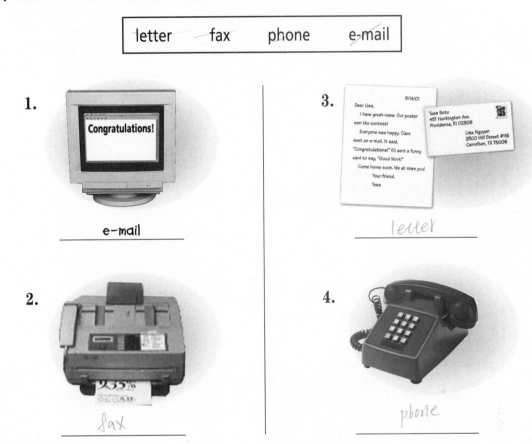

1. e-mail

2. fax

3. letter

4. phone

USE THE TELEPHONE

You call Sam on the phone. Write what you say.

5. **You:** Hi, Sam. This is _Hui-Chuan Chen_ .
   Sam: Hello. How are you?

6. **You:** I am fine, thanks. How can I order a school _phone_ ?
   Sam: Send me an e-mail.

7. **You:** I don't have e-mail. Can I send you a _letter_ ?
   Sam: Sure. Tell the size and color you need.

8. **You:** Okay. Thanks for your help. _Bye_ !
   Sam: You're welcome. See you tomorrow!

© Hampton-Brown

STATEMENTS AND EXCLAMATIONS

Everything Is New!

Some sentences tell something. Other sentences show a strong feeling.

This sentence tells something. It ends with a period.

Vu has a new jacket**.**

All sentences start with a capital letter.

She goes to a new school today.

This sentence shows a strong feeling. It ends with an exclamation mark.

She loves it **!**

Complete each sentence. Start each sentence with a capital letter. Add a period or an exclamation mark at the end.

1. ___Vu___ opens her new locker.
   (vu)

2. It is very small __.__

3. She puts her jacket in it __.__

4. Vu meets her new teacher __.__

5. ___He___ teaches English.
   (he)

6. He is very tall __.__

7. Vu walks home __.__

8. ___She___ sees snow for the first time.
   (she)

9. She loves the snow __.__

10. This is a great day __!__

WRITING PROJECT

Send a Postcard

**Send a message to a friend or relative. Write a postcard.
Follow these steps.**

1. Write the **date**.
Show the month,
day, and year.

2. Write a **greeting**.
Use *Dear* and your
friend's name.

3. Write your **message**.
Share your news.

Sept 10, 2011

Dear _____ Chang _____,

How are you? I am _fine, I study America Sign_
language and English at Gallaudet University.

I have news for you. I ____ am happy.

Love you, See you later.
Hui

Chang-Hsien Tsai

420 Girard St Apt 303 Gaithersburg

M MD 20877

4. Write a **closing** like
Love, See you soon,
or *Your friend.* Use
a comma after the
closing.

5. Write your name. That
is your **signature**.

6. Write your friend's **name** on the
first line. Write the street **address**
on the next line. Then write the
city, state, and zip code.

Copy your ideas onto a real postcard.

Mail your postcard. Don't forget to add a stamp!

VOCABULARY: COLORS, SHAPES, AND SIZES

Lunch Looks Good!

Look at each picture. Tell the size or shape. Use a word from the box.

small	round	square
long	triangular	rectangular

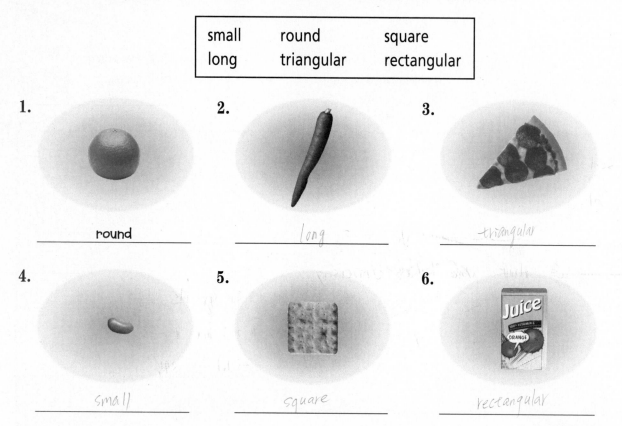

1. round

2. long

3. triangular

4. small

5. square

6. rectangular

DESCRIBE YOUR LUNCH

Complete the sentences. Add words to tell the color, size, or shape.

7. I eat pizza with my friends. We sit at

   a _____rectangular_____ table.

8. The pizza box has four equal sides. The box is ____square____ .

9. We do not eat a small pizza. We eat a ____triangular____ pizza.

10. The pizza is like a circle. It is ____triangular____ .

11. There is cheese on our pizza. The color is ____yellow____ , like a banana.

12. My slice of pizza is like a triangle. It is ____triangular____ .

VOCABULARY: FOODS

What's for Lunch?

Name each food. Use words from the box.

butter	milk	pear	roll
chicken	plum	peas 豌豆	water

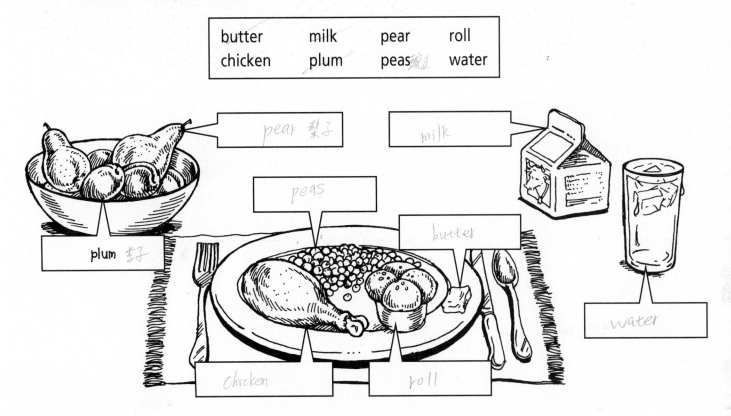

pear 梨子

milk

peas

butter

plum 李子

water

Chicken

roll

DESCRIBE THE FOOD

Complete each sentence. Tell about the food. Then name it.

1.
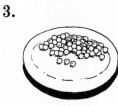
This is a kind of bread. You can put ___butter___ on it. It is a ___roll___ .

2.
This is a cold drink. It is in a tall ___cup___ . It is ___water___ .

3.

These are green. They are ___circle___ in size. They are ___peas___ .

4.

This is a fruit. It has a ___circle___ shape. It is a ___plum___ .

ACTION VERBS

Let's Eat Salad

An action verb tells what someone does.

I **make** tasty salads.

I **find** fresh lettuce.

I **take** a red tomato.

I **get** some carrots, too.

Complete each sentence. Tell how to make a salad. Use verbs from the box.

Action Verbs

wash	add	cut	put	eat	get

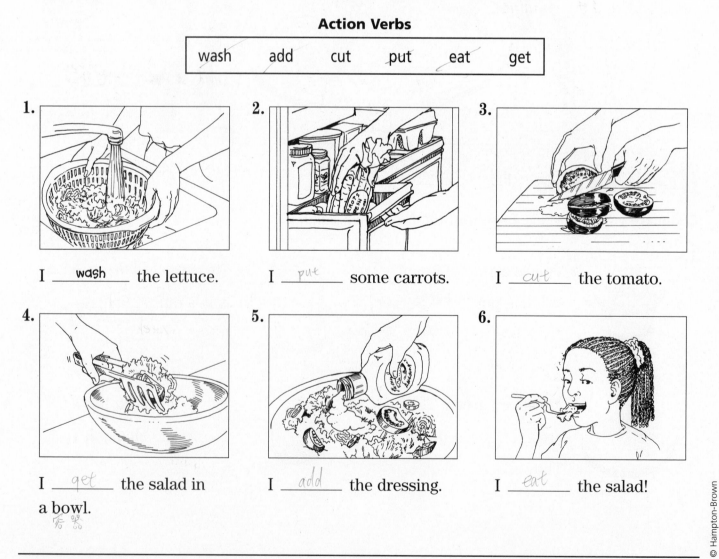

1. I __wash__ the lettuce.

2. I __put__ some carrots.

3. I __cut__ the tomato.

4. I __get__ the salad in a bowl.

5. I __add__ the dressing.

6. I __eat__ the salad!

NEGATIVE SENTENCES

I Am Not a Cook!

A negative sentence has a negative word, like *not*.

The fish is **not** big.

The carrots are **not** long.

Meg is **not** happy.

**Look at each picture. Complete the sentence.
Add a verb and the word *not*.**

1.

I ___*am*___ ___*not*___ a
good cook.

2.
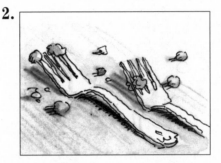

The forks ___*are*___ ___*not*___
clean.

3.

The plates ___*are*___ ___*not*___
on the table.

4.

The pasta ___*is*___ ___*not*___
in the water.

5.

The rolls ___*are*___ ___*not*___
hot.

6.

Dinner ___*is*___ ___*not*___
ready!

WRITING PROJECT: EXHIBIT CARD

Good Enough to Eat!

Tell your class how to make art with food. Draw a picture of the art you make. Then write a card. Follow these steps.

1. Draw a picture of your art.

2. Tell what your art is. Tell how you make it. Name each food. Describe the **color, size,** or **shape.** Tell the **steps in order**.

```
Picture
```

My art shows _____

_____ .

I use _____

_____ .

I cut _____

_____ .

I add _____

_____ .

Have a partner read your description. Did you tell all the steps?

Show your art and your card to the class.

© Hampton-Brown

Name _____ Date _____

Tell About the Jobs They Do

Study the charts.

Careers	Actions
artist	draw
cab driver	drive
carpenter 木匠	build 製作

Careers	Actions
gardener	plant 植物
police officer	protect 保護
teacher	teach

Complete each sentence. Use the chart.

1.

He is an ___artist___ .
He can ___draw___ and paint.

2.

She can ___build___ things.
She is a ___carpenter___ .

3.

Here is a ___gardener___ .
She can ___plant___ flowers.

4.

She can ___protect___ us.
She is a ___police offer___ .

5.

He is a ___teacher___ .
He can ___teach___ us how to write.

6.

This is a ___cab driver___ .
He can ___drive___ people places.

© Hampton-Brown

PRESENT TENSE VERBS

Everyone Helps

To tell what another person or thing does, use a verb that ends in -s.

The Ali family **owns** a store.

It **keeps** them busy.

Mr. Ali **works** hard.

Mrs. Ali **helps**.

Read each sentence. Add the correct form of the action verb.

1.

Mr. Ali _____cleans_____ .
(clean)

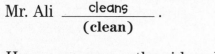

He _____ the sidewalk.
(sweep)

2.

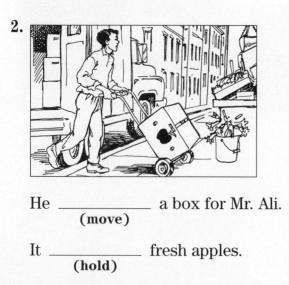

He _____ a box for Mr. Ali.
(move)

It _____ fresh apples.
(hold)

3.

Mrs. Ali _____ the money.
(take)

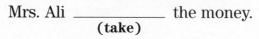

She _____ the man.
(thank)

4.

Kira _____ a flower.
(cut)

She _____ it in water.
(put)

VOCABULARY: TOOLS AND CAREERS

What Tools Do They Use?

Name the tool each worker has. Use words from the box.

| brush | pencil | notebook | wrench | paper | computer | scissors |

ANSWER QUESTIONS

Look at the pictures above. Read each question. Write the answer.

1. Can the artist draw?

Yes, she can.

2. Is the writer in an office?

Yes, she can.

3. Are the stylist and the boy in a garage?

No, they aren't.

4. Is the notebook open?

_____

5. Can the mechanic use a wrench?

_____

6. Is the wrench on the floor?

_____

QUESTIONS WITH *WHO?*, *WHAT?*, *WHERE?*, AND *WHEN?*

Who? What? Where? When?

You can use the words *Who*, *What*, *Where*, or *When* to start a question.

Use *Who* to ask about a person.

    Who is this?

Use *What* to ask about a thing.

    What is his job?

Use *Where* to ask about a place.

    Where can he go?

Use *When* to ask about a time.

    When is he at work?

Complete each question. Use *Who*, *What*, *Where*, or *When*.

1. _____Who_____ drives the cab?
   Mr. Siwela drives the cab.

2. _____ is on his head?
   A cap is on his head.

3. _____ is the cab?
   The cab is at the flower shop.

4. _____ is the shop?
   The shop is on Main Street.

5. _____ wants a ride in the cab?
   Ms. Vega wants a ride.

6. _____ is in her hand?
   A plant is in her hand.

7. _____ is she ready to go?
   She is ready to go now.

8. _____ is her home?
   Her home is on Elm Street.

What Is Your Job?

Interview a worker. Write a job report for a class handbook.
Follow these steps.

1. Study the questions
and answers from
your interview.

2. Name the worker's
job. Add a picture
of the worker.

3. Copy each **question**
and **answer** from
your interview. End
each question with
a **question mark**.

_____

What is _____

   My name is _____

_____

Where do _____

   I work _____

_____

What is _____

   I am _____

_____

What do _____

   I like _____

_____

Add your report to a class handbook.

QUESTIONS WITH *DO* AND *DOES*

What Questions Do They Ask?

Complete each question. Then complete the answer. Use *Do* or *Does*.

Questions with *Do* and *Does*

Use *do* with *I, you, we,* and *they.*
Do you have three caps?

Use *does* with *he, she,* and *it.*
Does she need two bags?

1. ___Do___ I need two caps?

No, you _____ not.

2. _____ you have five bats?

Yes, we _____.

3. _____ it cost ten dollars?

Yes, it _____.

4. _____ Marco work here?

No, he _____ not.

© Hampton-Brown

VOCABULARY: CARDINAL NUMBERS

Numbers Tell How Many

Read the number words. Write the numbers.

1. four thousand, five hundred forty _____4,540_____

2. nine hundred ninety-seven _____

3. three hundred ten thousand _____

4. two million, one hundred thousand _____

5. fifty-four thousand, one hundred one _____

6. eight hundred thirty-eight _____

7. five thousand, six hundred fourteen _____

8. seven hundred nineteen _____

9. thirty million, two hundred thousand _____

10. ten thousand, four hundred one _____

GIVE INFORMATION

Complete the facts about Fred's school. Use number words.

11. My school _has three fields_____.
    (3 fields)

12. My school _____.
    (12 classrooms)

13. My school _____.
    (24 computers)

    _____.

14. My school _____.
    (347 students)

    _____.

NEGATIVE SENTENCES

I Am Not Ready!

There are different ways to build negative sentences.

Add *not* after *am*, *is*, or *are*.

He is ready.   He is not ready.

Add *do not* or *does not* before other verbs.

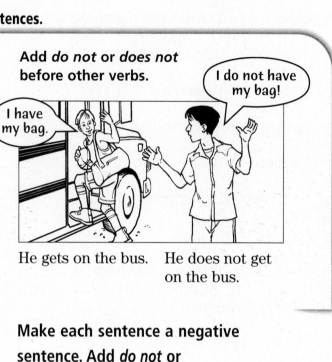

He gets on the bus.   He does not get on the bus.

Make each sentence a negative sentence. Use a verb and the word *not*.

1. I am ready for the game.

   I ___am not___ ready for the game.

2. The bus is on time.

   The bus _____ on time.

3. We are on Bus 5.

   We _____ on Bus 5.

Make each sentence a negative sentence. Add *do not* or *does not*.

4. The bus driver leaves at 4:00.

   The bus driver ___does not leave___ at 4:00.

5. She closes the doors.

   She _____ the doors.

6. The players go to the game.

   The players _____ to the game.

© Hampton-Brown

First, Second, Third…

Look at the picture. In what order are the people?
Write words from the box to show the order.

first	second	third	fourth	fifth
sixth	seventh	eighth	ninth	tenth

EXPRESS NEEDS

Use the picture above to complete each sentence.
Tell what the person needs.

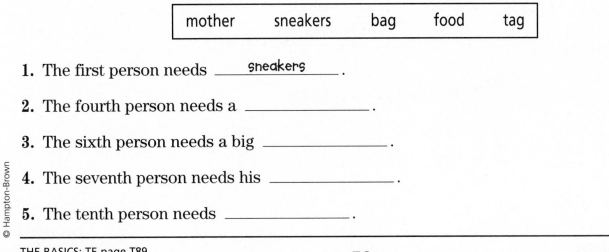

mother	sneakers	bag	food	tag

1. The first person needs _____sneakers_____ .

2. The fourth person needs a _____ .

3. The sixth person needs a big _____ .

4. The seventh person needs his _____ .

5. The tenth person needs _____ .

CONTRACTIONS WITH *NOT*

I Don't Want This Food!

When you make a contraction, you join two words together.

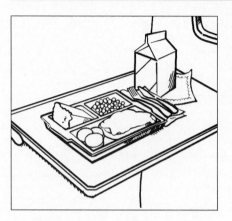

is + not = isn't	do + not = don't
are + not = aren't	does + not = doesn't

Use these contractions in negative sentences.

The food on the plane **isn't** very good.

The cookies **aren't** big.

The cake **doesn't** have nuts.

I **don't** want anything to eat.

Read each sentence. Change the <u>underlined</u> words to a contraction. Then complete the new sentence.

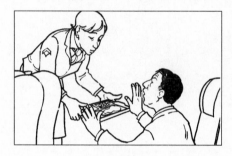

1. He <u>is not</u> happy.

He _____isn't_____ happy.

2. He <u>does not</u> like the food.

He _____ like the food.

3. She <u>does not</u> eat the cake.

She _____ eat the cake.

4. The cake <u>is not</u> sweet.

The cake _____ sweet.

5. They <u>do not</u> want to eat.

They _____ want to eat.

6. They <u>are not</u> hungry.

They _____ hungry.

WRITING PROJECT: FACT SHEET

Facts About a Country

Find number facts about a country. Take notes.
Then write a fact sheet for your class. Follow these steps.

1. Write the name of the **country.** Draw a map of the country if you want to.

2. Write a **research question**. Give the answer.
  - Use **facts and numbers** from your notes.
  - Use complete sentences.

3. Write the rest of your research questions and answers.

4. Check your questions and answers. Did you use capital letters for the names of places? Are the commas in the numbers in the right places?

- How large is

  The country of

  is

- What is the

- What is the

A map of

_____

Share your fact sheet with your class.

© Hampton-Brown

VOCABULARY: LOCATION WORDS

Where Is It?

Study the places.

Location Words

in
on
by, near
above, over
below, under
next to, beside
between
down
behind, in back of

Complete each sentence. Tell where the places are.
Use location words.

1. The pet shop is _____ on _____ the corner.

2. You can get dog food _____ the pet shop.

3. The toy store is _____ the café.

4. The toy store is _____ the music store and the market.

5. You go _____ the stairs to get from the market to the bakery.

6. The market is _____ the bakery.

7. The café is _____ the bakery.

8. There are two plants _____ the café.

9. There is someone _____ the door to the bakery.

10. The theater is _____ the pet shop.

Things in the Neighborhood

Name each place. Then name something you see there. Use words from the box.

| intersection | post office | bus station | store |
| bus | parking lot | mailbox | stop sign |

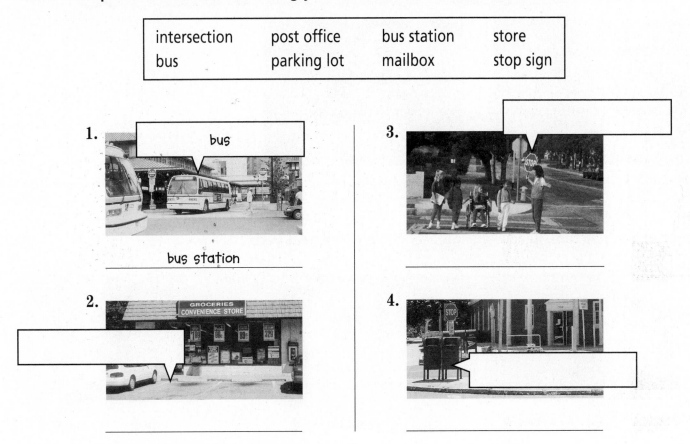

1. **bus**

bus station

2.

3.

4.

ASK FOR AND GIVE INFORMATION

Answer each question. Use a complete sentence.

5. What happens at the bus station?

    People wait for the bus.

6. What happens at the intersection?

    _____

7. What happens at the store?

    _____

8. What happens at the post office?

    _____

REGULAR PAST TENSE VERBS

On My Street

A verb changes to show the past tense.

She **cooks** the food.

She **cooked** the food.

Look at each picture. Read the sentence. Circle the correct verb.

1.

They ____ play / (played) ____ soccer.

2.

She ____ parks / parked ____ her car.

3.

He ____ opens / opened ____ the bag of chips.

4.

She ____ adds / added ____ flowers to the garden.

5.

He ____ cleans / cleaned ____ the car.

6.

They ____ help / helped ____ win the game.

REGULAR PAST TENSE VERBS

We Visited the Zoo

You can add –ed to many verbs to tell about things that happened in the past.

We **wanted** to go to the city zoo.

I **asked** Mom to take us there.

Complete each sentence. Add the past tense of the verb in dark type.

1. We ____walked____ around the zoo.
   (walk)

2. Sam _____ the young lions.
   (like)

3. They _____ so big!
   (look)

4. Tara _____ away from them!
   (stay)

5. I _____ to see the monkeys.
   (ask)

6. They _____ all around.
   (jump)

7. One monkey _____ a ball.
   (toss)

8. We _____ to them yell!
   (listen)

9. Mom _____ .
   (laugh)

10. We all _____ our visit.
    (enjoy)

STATEMENTS WITH *THERE IS* AND *THERE ARE*

What Is in the Library?

You can start a sentence with *There is* or *There are*.

Use *There is* to talk about one person or thing.

There is a flag by the library.

Use *There are* to talk about two or more persons or things.

There are trees by the library, too.

Complete each sentence. Tell about each photo. Add *There is* or *There are*.

1. _____There is_____ a lamp on the desk.

2. _____ a pencil by the lamp.

3. _____ books in the box.

4. _____ a librarian behind the desk.

5. _____ many books on the bookshelf.

6. _____ a window in the library.

7. _____ a girl beside the window.

8. _____ two students at the table.

PRONOUN-VERB CONTRACTIONS

They're from My Neighborhood

You can put a pronoun and a verb together to form a contraction.

Contraction	Example
I + am = I'm	**I'm** on the sidewalk.
you + are = you're	**You're** slow!
he + is = he's she + is = she's it + is = it's	**It's** a sunny day.
we + are = we're	**We're** glad to be together.
they + are = they're	**They're** in the park.

Combine the words in dark type to make a contraction.

Use the contraction to complete the sentence.

1. Sam and Kim are Mia's friends. _____They're_____ her neighbors.
(They are)

2. Mia walks the dogs for Sam and Kim. _____ happy to do it.
(She is)

3. One dog stops to rest. _____ a small dog.
(He is)

4. Mia laughs at the dog. "_____ slow, Biff."
(You are)

5. "You can rest, Biff. _____ not in a hurry."
(We are)

6. Mia waits for Biff. _____ nice to all the dogs.
(She is)

7. People look at the dogs. _____ surprised to see so many!
(They are)

8. Soon the walk is over. _____ time to eat.
(It is)

WRITING PROJECT: JOURNAL ENTRY

A Week in My City

Tell what you did last week. Make a detail chart.
Then write a journal entry. Follow these steps.

1. Write today's **date**.

2. Now write a sentence for each day last week. Tell what you did. Tell where you did it. Use **past tense** verbs.

Last Monday, I

On Tuesday,

On Wednesday,

On Thursday,

On Friday,

On Saturday,

On Sunday,

3. Add drawings or photos.

© Hampton-Brown

VOCABULARY: FAMILY

Meet Lin's Family

Use family words to tell about Lin's family tree.
Then answer the question below.

Family Words

grandfather	grandmother
father	mother
brother	sister
uncle	aunt

grandfather   g randmother   grandfather   grandmother

father   mother

brother   Lin   sister

Lin's Family Tree

How many people are in Lin's family?

_____ of them together

Make up Lin's family tree.

PRESENT TENSE VERBS: *HAS* AND *HAVE*

I Have a Great Family

Use *have* with *I, you, we,* and *they.* Use *has* with *he, she,* or *it.*

Hi. I'm Rita. I **have** a sister. We **have** a new brother. He **has** a room. It **has** toys in it.

Complete each sentence. Use *have* or *has*.

1.

"I ___have___ an aunt."

"She ___has___ a dog."

2.

"We ___have___ a small house."

"The house ___has___ trees around it."

3.

He ___has___ a sister.

They ___have___ fun together.

4.

He ___has___ an uncle.

His uncle ___has___ a big bike.

VOCABULARY: HOUSEHOLD OBJECTS

What Is in Each Room?

Name the things in each room. Use words from the box.

bathtub	couch	curtains	bed	dresser	rug
lamp	sink	refrigerator	oven	shower	door

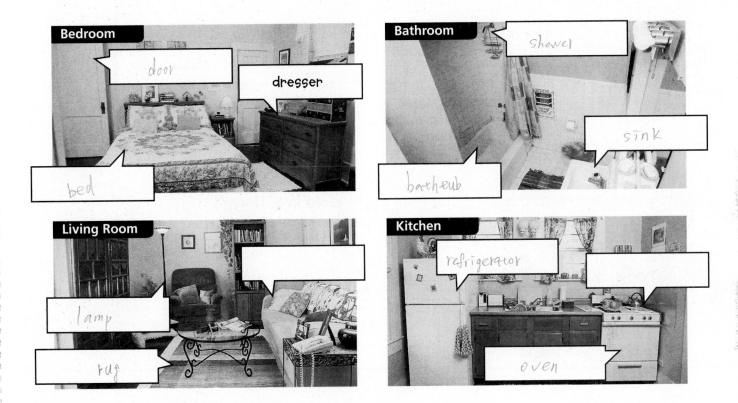

Bedroom
door
dresser
bed

Bathroom
shower
sink
bathtub

Living Room
lamp
rug

Kitchen
refrigerator
oven

ASK AND ANSWER QUESTIONS

Answer each question. Use a complete sentence.

1. Where is the couch? The couch is in the living room.

2. Where is the dresser? The dresser is in the bedroom.

3. Where is the oven? The oven is in the kitchen.

Write two questions. Ask about two things in the rooms above.

4. Where is the lamp? The lamp is in the living room.

5. Where is the shower? The shower is in the bathroom.

PLURAL NOUNS

New Neighbors

A noun names a person, place, or thing.

A singular noun names one thing.

box

A plural noun names more than one thing.

boxes

Study these rules for forming plurals.

To make most nouns plural, just add -*s*.	boy boys	girl girls	book books
If the noun ends in *x*, *ch*, *sh*, *s*, or *z*, add -*es*.	box boxes	dish dishes	glass glasses
Some nouns change in different ways to show the plural.	man men	woman women	child children

Complete each sentence. Use the plural form of the word in dark type.

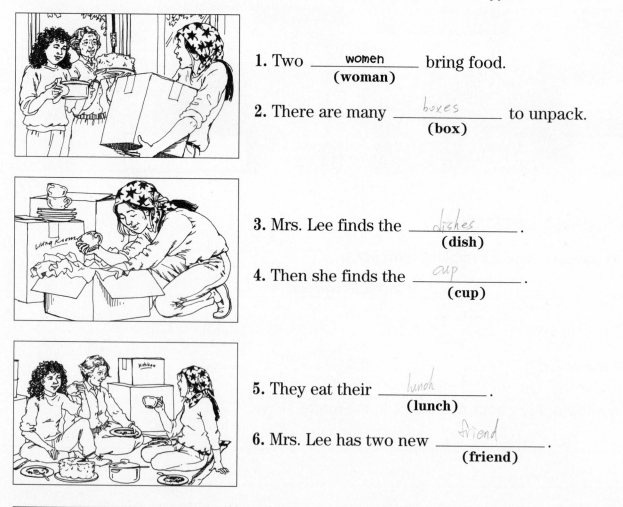

1. Two _____women_____ bring food.
   (woman)

2. There are many ___boxes___ to unpack.
   (box)

3. Mrs. Lee finds the ___dishes___.
   (dish)

4. Then she finds the ___cup___.
   (cup)

5. They eat their ___lunch___.
   (lunch)

6. Mrs. Lee has two new ___friend___.
   (friend)

My Family

Tell your class about your family. Make a chart. Then make
a page for a family album. Follow these steps.

1. Write a title and
   your **name**.

   by _____

2. Choose a person
   from your chart.
   Write two
   sentences about
   the person. Use
   plural nouns.

3. Draw a picture to
   show something
   the person likes
   or has.

4. Tell about
   another person
   in your family.
   Add another
   drawing.

Make more pages about other people in your family.

Display your family album in your classroom.

COMMANDS

Give Commands

Study the commands.

Wear a jacket.	Get some warm clothes.	Find a seat.
Grab a camera.	Ride the bus.	Pack your bag.
Enjoy the trip!	Take some gloves.	Step on the bus.
Dress for snow.	Don't forget a hat.	Take some film.

> **Commands**
>
> A **command** tells you what to do or what not to do.
>
> **Pack** your bags.
> **Don't forget**.

Write two commands for each picture.
Use commands from the box.

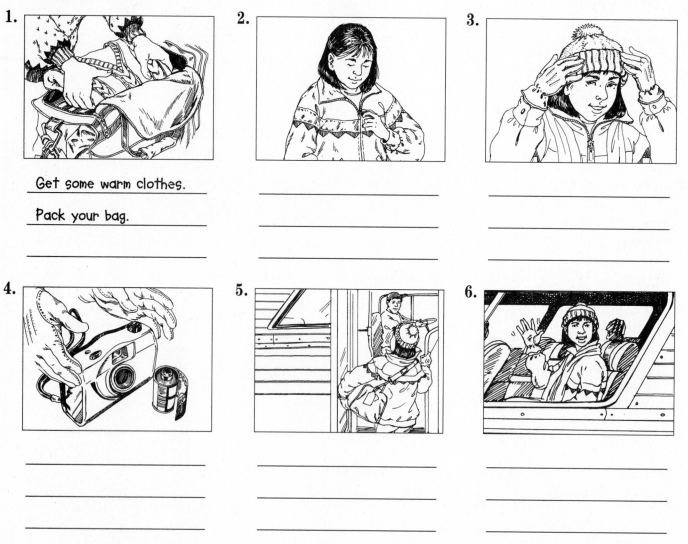

1.

Get some warm clothes.

Pack your bag.

_____

2.

_____

_____

_____

3.

_____

_____

_____

4.

_____

_____

_____

5.

_____

_____

_____

6.

_____

_____

_____

What Do You See?

Name the places and things in the picture. Use words from the box.

ocean	sailboat	beach
forest	airplane	island

island

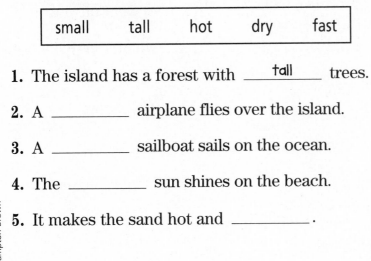

DESCRIBE A PLACE

Complete each sentence. Describe the picture above.
Use adjectives from the box.

small	tall	hot	dry	fast

1. The island has a forest with ____tall____ trees.

2. A _____ airplane flies over the island.

3. A _____ sailboat sails on the ocean.

4. The _____ sun shines on the beach.

5. It makes the sand hot and _____ .

VOCABULARY: WEATHER AND CLOTHING

What Do They Wear?

Name the things to wear. Use words from the box.

| sneaker | glove | scarf | bathing suit | sandal | parka |

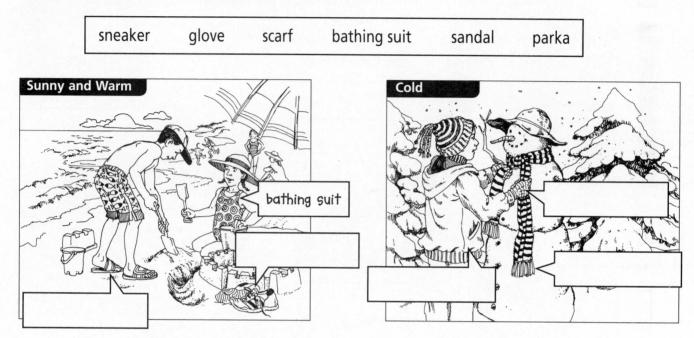

Sunny and Warm

bathing suit

Cold

GIVE INFORMATION

What is the weather like? Tell Brandon and Rachel what clothing to pack.

1. It is _____ sunny _____ and _____ warm _____ at the beach.

2. Take a _____ so you can swim.

3. Pack some _____ to wear on your feet.

4. Wear your _____ when it is really hot.

5. It is _____ in the mountains.

6. Take a warm coat or _____ .

7. Pack _____ to keep your hands warm.

8. Wear a _____ around your neck.

© Hampton-Brown

VERBS: CAN

Yes, You Can!

Use *can* before another verb to tell what people are able to do.

can + sail = can sail

My father **can sail** a boat.

He **can take** my sister to an island.

She **can visit** her friends there.

Never add *-s* to *can*.

Complete each sentence. Tell what the people in each picture can do. Use *can* and a word from the box.

| work | wear | see | hike | ski | play | plant | swim |

winter   spring   summer   fall

1. In the winter, he _____can ski_____ in the mountains.

2. In the winter, he _____ in the snow.

3. In the spring, she _____ in the garden.

4. In the spring, she _____ flowers.

5. In the summer, he _____ in the pool.

6. In the summer, he _____ a bathing suit.

7. In the fall, they _____ pretty trees.

8. In the fall, they _____ in the park.

Special Places, Special People

A proper noun names one particular person, place, or thing.

A proper noun begins with a <u>capital letter</u>.

name of a person	**Sabrina** helps kids at a summer camp.
name of a special place, a city, or a country	She works at **Camp Bellwood** in **Cloverdale**, **New York**.
name of a month or a day	Camp begins on **Saturday**, **June** 30.

Read each sentence. Circle the letters that should be capital letters.

1. Camp (b)ellwood is in (c)loverdale, New York.
2. It is near sutter mountain.
3. Many campers come from boston, massachusetts.
4. They learn to swim at lake bronson.
5. Their teacher is mindy lee.
6. Sabrina and jamal take campers on a hike through the forest.
7. There is a big party at camp on thursday, july 4.
8. On Wednesday, july 10, the campers visit Joe taylor at his farm.
9. The next week, Jamal takes them to niagara Falls.
10. Everyone is sorry when camp ends on friday, august 2.

WRITING PROJECT: CLASS TRAVEL BOOK

Explore the World!

Find information about a place. Take notes on a concept map.

Use your notes to write a page for a class travel book.

Tell how to get to the place. Write the name of the **country**. Use a **capital letter**.

Tell what you can see and hear at the place. Write complete sentences.

Add pictures to your page.

Take _____ .

Explore _____ !

You can see _____

_____

_____

_____

_____ .

You can hear _____

_____

_____

_____

_____

_____ .

Read your page to the class.

Add your page to the class travel book.

REGULAR PAST TENSE VERBS

They Cooked Pizza Together

Complete each sentence. Tell what the friends did.
Use a verb from the box.

laughed	helped	spilled	rolled
enjoyed	looked	cooked	watched

> **Past Tense Verbs**
>
> The **past tense** of a verb tells about an action in the past. Many past tense verbs end in **-ed**.
>
> Len scratch**ed** his head.

1.

Miguel _____rolled_____ the dough.

Len _____watched_____ at the cookbook.

2.

Miguel _____spilled_____ sauce.

Len _____helped_____ about the mess.

3.

Then Len _____looked_____ with the

dough. Miguel _____enjoyed_____ him.

4.

Finally, the boys _____cooked_____

the pizza. They _____laughed_____

their dinner.

VOCABULARY: FEELINGS

How Do They Feel?

Look at each picture. Tell how the person feels.
Use a word from the box.

害怕的	困惑の	厭煩の	生氣の	得意の	信心
scared	confused	bored	mad	proud	sad

1. confused

2. mad

3. sad

4. scared

5. bored

6. proud

EXPRESS FEELINGS

Read each sentence. Tell how you feel.

7. I get a good grade on my test.

   I feel ___proud___.

8. My best friend moves to another city.

   I am ___sad___.

9. There is nothing for me to do. 沒有任何東西

   I feel ___confused___.

10. A bee buzzes around my head.

    I am ___scared___.

IRREGULAR PAST TENSE VERBS: *WAS* AND *WERE*

It Was Fun to Study Together

Use *was* and *were* to tell about the past.

Pronoun	Verb	Example
I	was	I **was** in the library.
you	were	You **were** by the bookshelf.
he, she, it	was	It **was** warm in the library.
we	were	We **were** not bored.
they	were	They **were** curious about the magazines.

Use *There was* for one person or thing.
Use *There were* for two or more.

> **There was** a girl beside me.
> **There were** many books to read.

Complete each sentence. Use *was* or *were*.

1. It ___was___ 1:30.

2. I ___was___ with my friends.

3. We ___were___ in the library.

4. Other students ___were___ there, too.

5. There ___was___ a new librarian at the desk.

6. Our table ___was___ not very big.

7. Carol ___was___ beside me.

8. There ___was___ good magazines on the shelf.

9. Mr. Smith ___was___ glad to answer my questions.

10. It ___was___ fun to study with my friends.

NEGATIVE SENTENCES AND CONTRACTIONS WITH *NOT*

We Weren't There!

There are different ways to build negative sentences in the past tense.

Add the word *not* after *was* and *were*.

She **was not** happy.
We **were not** on time.

With other verbs, add *did not* <u>before</u> the verb.

did not
The movie started.

> When you add *did not* to a sentence, take the *-ed* off the main verb.

Complete the sentence. Use *did not*, *was not*, or *were not*. Then write the sentence. Use a contraction.

Contractions

did + not = didn't
was + not = wasn't
were + not = weren't

1. Kelli ____was not____ late.

   Kelli wasn't late.

2. Dina and I ____were not____ there.

   Dina and I weren't there

3. We ____were not____ answer the phone.

   We weren't answer the phone.

4. The bus ____was not____ stop for us.

   The bus wasn't stop for us.

5. We ____were not____ on time for the movie.

   We weren't on time for the movie.

6. Kelli ____was not____ happy.

   kelli wasn't happy

POSSESSIVE NOUNS

Meg's Friends

Some nouns show ownership. They end in 's.

Meg**'s** best friend is Helen. Helen**'s** family lives next door. Helen has a brother. Her brother**'s** name is Fred.

Complete each sentence. Add 's to the word in dark print.

1. ___Meg's___ favorite sport is tennis.
   (Meg)

2. Her ___friend's___ favorite game is tennis, too.
   (friend)

3. Meg uses her ___dad's___ racket to play tennis.
   (dad)

4. Helen borrows her ___brother's___ racket.
   (brother)

5. ___Fred's___ racket is new.
   (Fred)

6. ___Helen's___ mom and dad take the girls
   (Helen)
   to the park.

7. They play tennis in the ___city's___ park.
   (city)

8. Then ___Helen's___ brother brings the girls home.
   (Helen)

© Hampton-Brown

WRITING PROJECT: FRIENDSHIP BOOK

A Special Time with Friends

Write a page for a friendship book. Make a chart to plan
your page. Then write about a day with a friend. Follow these steps.

1. Write a **title**
   and your name.

2. Tell the **names**
   of your friends
   in the first
   sentence.

3. Tell what you
   did. Use verbs
   in the **past
   tense**. Tell how
   you felt. Use
   feeling words.

4. Add pictures.
   Tell about
   each picture.

by Hui

Dear sweet Chang
Hello! How are you?
I studies English and America Sign in Gallaudet
University now.

Put your page on construction paper.
Add it to a class friendship book.

ADVERBS

How Does He Dance?

Look at each picture. Answer the question.
Use an adverb from the box.

up	back	high	slowly	forward	now

> **Adverbs**
>
> Many **adverbs** end in **-ly**. They tell how:
> turn **quickly**
> dance **wildly**
> Other adverbs tell when or where:
> dance **now**
> step **back**

1.

Where does Matt stretch?

Matt stretches _____up_____ .

2.

How does Matt bend?

Matt bends _____slowly_____ .

3.

Can Matt jump?

Yes, Matt can jump _____high_____ .

4.

Where does Matt reach?

He reaches _____forward_____ .

5.

Can Matt go back?

No, Matt can't go _____back_____ .

6.

When can he dance?

He can dance _____now_____ !

PRESENT PROGRESSIVE VERBS

What Are They Doing?

These verbs tell what is happening now.

The girls **are celebrating** their culture.

They **are standing** in line.

The powwow **is starting** soon.

Complete each sentence. Tell what the people are doing.
Use verbs from the box.

is listening	are moving	is singing	is stepping
are sitting	are enjoying	is hopping 跳 躍	are playing

1. The dancer _____is stepping_____ quickly.

2. His feet _____are moving_____ forward. 向前

3. He _____is hopping_____ up and down.

4. He _____is listening_____ to the music.

5. The children _____are sitting_____ in a circle.

6. They _____are playing_____ the drums. 鼓

7. One boy _____is singing_____ a song. 歌曲

8. The children _____are enjoying_____ the music.

© Hampton-Brown

VOCABULARY: COUNTRY WORDS

Dancers Around the World

Look at each picture. Complete the sentences. Use words from the box.

Scotland	Scottish	Cambodia	Cambodian

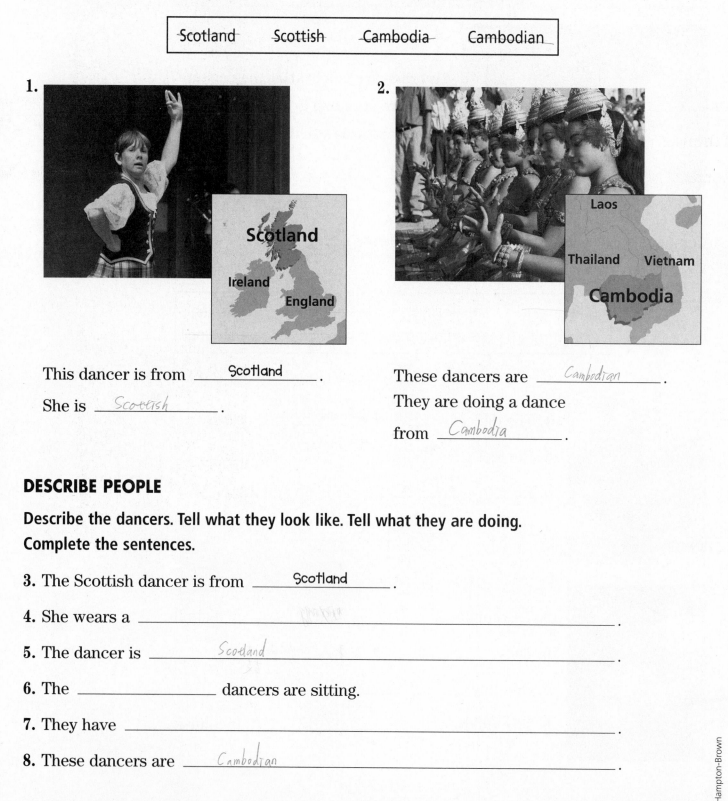

1.

This dancer is from _____Scotland_____.
She is _____Scottish_____.

2.

These dancers are _____Cambodian_____.
They are doing a dance
from _____Cambodia_____.

DESCRIBE PEOPLE

Describe the dancers. Tell what they look like. Tell what they are doing.
Complete the sentences.

3. The Scottish dancer is from _____Scotland_____.

4. She wears a _____.

5. The dancer is _____Scotland_____.

6. The _____ dancers are sitting.

7. They have _____.

8. These dancers are _____Cambodian_____.

© Hampton–Brown

PHRASES WITH *LIKE TO* AND *WANT TO*

We Like to Dance!

Use a verb to complete a phrase with *like to* or *want to*.

| like to | + | verb |

They **like to dance** together.
She **likes to step** to the music.

| want to | + | verb |

They **want to learn** more steps.
He **wants to teach** people.

Add an _-s_ when you use *he*, *she*, or *it*.

Complete the sentences for each picture. Use *like to* or *want to*.

1.

The students ____like to____ leap.
They ____like to____ perform for the Russian ballet.

2.

The boy ____wants to____ spin.
He ____wants to____ dance fast.

3.

The boys ____likes to____ celebrate the Chinese New Year.
They ____like to____ carry the dragon costume.

4.

The dancer from India ____wants to____ share a story.
She ____wants to____ show it with her dance.

© Hampton-Brown

WRITING PROJECT: CELEBRATION POSTER

A Cultural Celebration

Make a poster for your class. Interview someone in your family.
Then use your notes to tell about a family celebration.
Follow these steps.

1. Name the
celebration.

_____

_____

2. Add pictures.
Show what you
do at the
celebration.
Show what you
wear or eat.

_____

_____

_____

_____

3. Write sentences.
Tell what is
happening in
each picture.
Use **verbs**
with *-ing*.

_____

_____

_____

_____

Check your work. Make it into a poster.
Tell your class about your poster.

VERBS: MAY, MIGHT, COULD

I Could Help

Complete each sentence. Tell about the job Jim could have.
Use words from the box.

may meet	might be	could take
could go	might carry	could fight
might save	may drive	may rescue

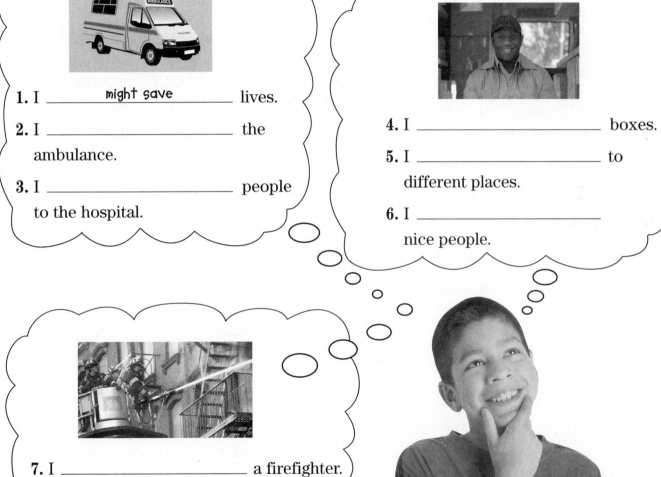

1. I _____might save_____ lives.

2. I _____ the ambulance.

3. I _____ people to the hospital.

4. I _____ boxes.

5. I _____ to different places.

6. I _____ nice people.

7. I _____ a firefighter.

8. I _____ fires.

9. I _____ people.

© Hampton-Brown

VOCABULARY: TIME

What Time Is It?

Look at each clock. Write the time. Use words from the box.

| ten to five | nine o'clock | eleven fifteen | noon | two thirty | quarter after six |

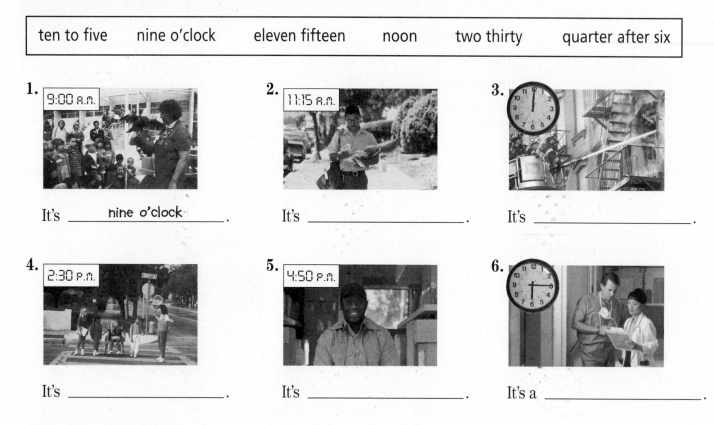

1. It's _____nine o'clock_____ .

2. It's _____ .

3. It's _____ .

4. It's _____ .

5. It's _____ .

6. It's a _____ .

TELL WHAT MAY HAPPEN

Look at each picture above. Tell what may happen at that time.

7. Mrs. Patch ___may teach children about other birds_____ .

8. The mail carrier _____ .

9. The firefighters _____ .

10. The crossing guard _____ .

11. The delivery man _____ .

12. The doctors _____ .

We Have to Help!

Use a verb to complete a phrase with *have to* or *need to*.

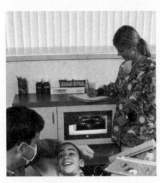

have to	+	verb

They **have to work** together.
She **has to help** the dentist.

Use *has* with *he, she,* or *it*.

need to	+	verb

They **need to wear** masks.
He **needs to use** tools.

Use *needs* with *he, she,* or *it*.

Complete each sentence. Circle the correct form of *have to* or *need to*.

1. They ___(need to)/ needs to___ fix the road.

2. They ___need to / needs to___ help each other.

3. They ___has to / have to___ wear hard hats.

4. She ___need to / needs to___ stop traffic.

5. He ___has to / have to___ deliver the mail.

6. He ___need to / needs to___ check the address.

7. It ___has to / have to___ show the person's name.

8. He ___need to / needs to___ take the letter to the right place.

POSSESSIVE PRONOUNS

What Is Your Job?

These pronouns tell who or what owns something.

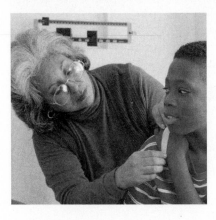

Pronoun	Example
my	I help **my** patients.
your	**Your** friend Ben is one of my patients.
his	**His** sister visited him yesterday.
her	She talked to **her** brother.
its	This bed moves. It rolls on **its** wheels.
our	We will take Ben to **our** operating room.
your	Will you visit **your** friend later?
their	His parents are here to see **their** son.

Read each sentence. Add the missing pronoun.

1. We have many patients in _____our_____ hospital.

2. I am a nurse. I enjoy helping _____ patients.

3. An ambulance is coming. I hear _____ sirens.

4. This young man fell off _____ bike and hurt his leg.

5. "Does _____ leg feel better now, Jim?"

6. "Yes, _____ leg feels fine," he says.

7. His parents are here. They want to see

   _____ son.

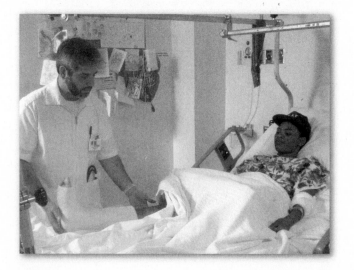

8. Jim's mom is glad. _____ son will be
   all right.

We Need This Worker

Work with a partner. Write an ad for a job at your school. Follow these steps.

1. Choose a job. Write questions and answers about the job.

2. Look at your notes.
- **Name** the job. Tell what kind of worker you need.
- Add a **picture** to show something about the job.

3. Tell more about the job. Use **complete sentences**.
- Tell where the job is.
- Tell when the person needs to work.
- Explain what the worker has to do.

_____

_____

_____

_____

Come and work at _____

_____ .

You have to _____

_____ .

You could also _____

_____ .

Put your ad on a wall in your classroom.

Tell your classmates about the job.

IRREGULAR PAST TENSE VERBS

Tell Me About It

Read each sentence. Change the verb
in dark print to the past tense.
Write the sentence.

1. I **am** lost and alone.

   I was lost and alone.

2. I **feel** confused and worried.

   _____

3. A girl **speaks** to me.

   _____

4. She **comes** with me to the bus.

   _____

5. I **meet** her after school.

   _____

6. We **make** plans for the next day.

   _____

7. I **am** not lonely any more.

   _____

8. We **are** best friends!

   _____

Name _____   Date _____

We Help at the Playground

Study the picture.

Complete each sentence. Use a direction word from the box.

| up | around | down | across | into |

1. Janis walks ____around____ the sandbox.

2. Bill steps _____ the sandbox.

3. Kira goes _____ the slide.

4. Rico and Brad walk _____ the bridge.

5. May helps Jess go _____ the ladder.

GIVE DIRECTIONS

Read each sentence. Find the places in the picture above. Write the directions.

6. Tell how to get from the ground to the top of the slide.

   Stand at the bottom of the ladder. Go up the steps.

7. Tell how to get from the sandbox to the swings.

   _____

8. Tell the boys on the bridge how to get to the slide.

   _____
   _____

© Hampton-Brown

Work for Change

These people want to save an old house. What can they do?
Complete the sentences. Use words from the box.

banner	ballot	letters	vote	protest	print	sign	Internet

1. The people can _____protest_____ .

2. They can use a _____ or

   a _____ .

3. Adults can _____ .

4. They can use a _____

   in an election.

5. People can write _____ .

6. They can _____ their ideas in a newspaper.

7. They can publish ideas over the _____ , too.

EXPRESS WANTS AND FEELINGS

Answer each question. Write a complete sentence.

8. How do the people feel about the house? _____

_____

9. What do the protesters want others to do? _____

_____

They Gave People Hope

These verbs have special forms to tell about the past.

Frederick Douglass

Present	Past	Example
think	thought	Frederick Douglass **thought** slaves should be free.
lead	led	He **led** the movement to end slavery.
go	went	He **went** across America.
give	gave	He **gave** strong speeches.
speak	spoke	He **spoke** about equal rights.
see	saw	Many people **saw** him and agreed with him. In 1865, Congress passed a law to end slavery.

Complete each sentence. Use the past tense of the verb in dark print.

1. Eleanor Roosevelt _____thought_____ all people
   (think)

   should have the same rights.

2. She _____ a movement to get fair
   (lead)

   treatment for people everywhere.

3. Eleanor _____ around the world.
   (go)

4. She _____ with the leaders of many countries.
   (speak)

Eleanor Roosevelt

5. She _____ important speeches.
   (give)

6. People _____ her and agreed with her ideas.
   (see)

WRITING PROJECT: MANDALA

You Matter in the World

Tell how you helped someone. Make a chart to show your ideas.
Use one idea to make a mandala for your class. Follow these steps.

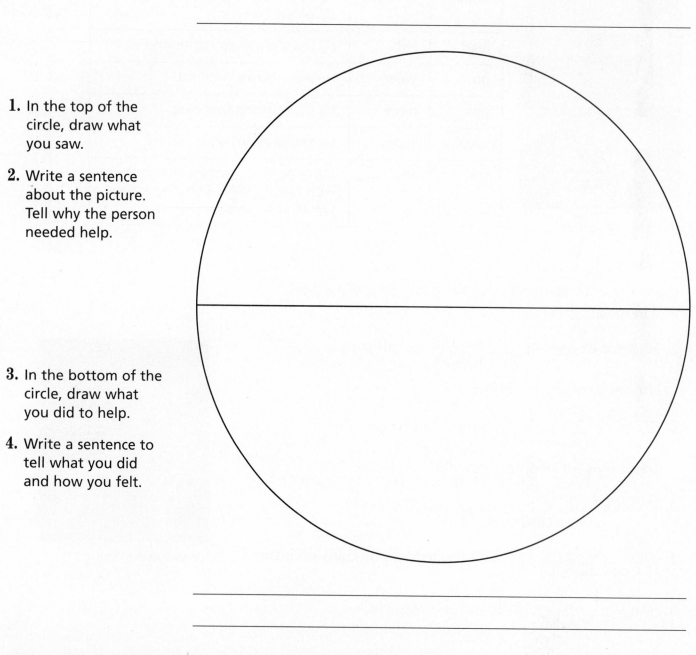

1. In the top of the circle, draw what you saw.

2. Write a sentence about the picture. Tell why the person needed help.

3. In the bottom of the circle, draw what you did to help.

4. Write a sentence to tell what you did and how you felt.

Copy your work onto colored paper. Decorate your mandala.
Then share it with your class.

VOCABULARY: OPINION WORDS

What Is Your Opinion?

Read the opinion. Then write your own opinion.
Use words from the box.

Opinion Words

People use these words to give an opinion.

must	**should**
think	**believe**

1.

Everyone should care for the Earth.

My Opinion: _I believe that everyone_
should care for the Earth.

2.

We must clean up our water.

My Opinion: _____

_____

3.

You should pick up trash.

My Opinion: _____

_____

4.

We should stop air pollution.

My Opinion: _____

_____

5.

We must protect the forest.

My Opinion: _____

_____

VOCABULARY: ANIMALS AND HABITATS

What Lives Around the Water?

Name what you can see in each place. Use the chart.

Seashore			Pond		
salt water	jellyfish	seal	frog	fish	turtle
starfish	seagull	crab	fresh water	duck	beaver

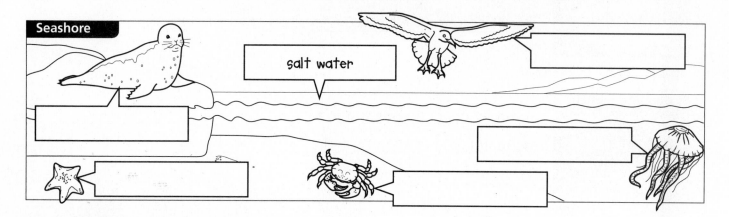

DESCRIBE PLACES

Complete each sentence. Describe the plants and animals above.
Add an adjective from Handbook page 310.

1. I see a _____ big seal _____ at the seashore.

   There is a _____ in the water.

2. I see a _____ in the pond.

   There is a _____ in the water.

© Hampton-Brown

Life in the Forest

Name the things in the pictures. Use words from the box.

branch	flower	tree	trunk
petal	soil	stem	undergrowth

Forest

tree

MAKE A SUGGESTION

What can you and your friends do in the forest? Make some suggestions.

1. Let's _take pictures with our cameras_____.

2. Would you like to go _____?

3. We could look _____.

4. Why don't we _____?

SENSORY ADJECTIVES

Describe the Earth

Adjectives can tell what something is like.

An adjective can tell how something **looks**.

The Joshua tree is **tall**.

An adjective can tell how something **sounds**.

A **loud** coyote is near the tree.

An adjective can tell how something **feels**.

The desert is **hot**.

Complete each sentence. Add an adjective from the box.
Tell how each thing looks, sounds, or feels.

Looks		Sounds		Feels	
tall	small	quiet	noisy	hard	hot

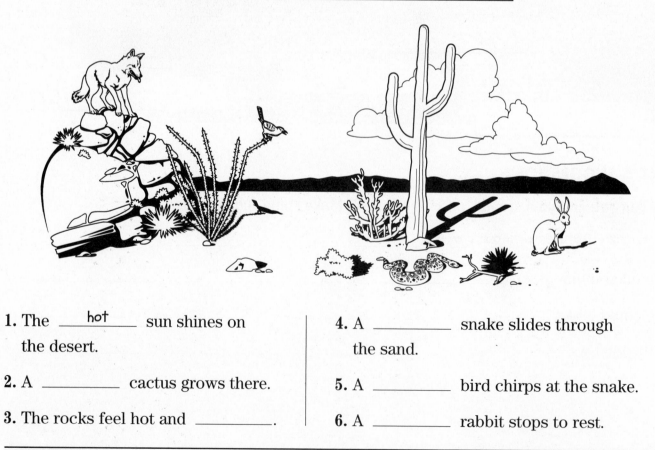

1. The ____hot____ sun shines on the desert.

2. A _____ cactus grows there.

3. The rocks feel hot and _____.

4. A _____ snake slides through the sand.

5. A _____ bird chirps at the snake.

6. A _____ rabbit stops to rest.

We Must Protect This Animal

**Find facts about an animal. Write the facts and your opinions in a chart.
Use your notes to make a poster for your class. Follow these steps.**

1. Start in the middle section. Name
the animal. Draw a picture of it.

2. Write a caption for your picture. Use
adjectives to describe the animal.

Facts:

_____

My Opinions:

_____

_____

_____

_____

_____

_____

The _____

is _____.

It _____

_____.

3. Write **facts** about the
animal in this section.

Put your work on heavy paper.

Share your poster with the class.

4. Write your opinions
about the animal in
this section. Use
opinion words like
think or *should*.

VOCABULARY: HISTORICAL RECORDS

How We Learn About the Past

Complete each sentence. Tell about the picture. Use words from the box.

| newspaper | historian | diary | history book | photographs |

1.

In a _____diary_____ you can read about what a person's life was like in the past.

2.

A _____ has _____ that make the news come alive.

3.

A _____ is written by a _____.

MAKE COMPARISONS

Complete each sentence. Compare the historical records.

4. Both a ____newspaper____ and a _____ give facts about events.

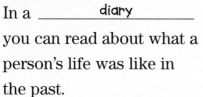

5. A _____ reports events as they happen, but a _____ reports events after they have happened.

6. A _____ tells about the events in one person's life, but a _____ tells about events in the lives of many people.

NOUNS

Person, Place, or Thing?

A noun names a person, place, or thing.

Rosie the Riveter stood for all the <u>women</u> who worked in
person   people

<u>factories</u> in <u>America</u> during <u>World War II</u>.
thing   place   thing

Rosie the Riveter

**Read each sentence. Tell if the underlined word
is a person, place, or thing.**

1. During <u>World War II</u>, many American men had to go to war.   _____thing_____

2. They went to <u>Europe</u>, Africa, and Asia.   _____

3. They had to leave their jobs in the <u>factories</u>.   _____

4. Soon <u>women</u> went to work in the factories.   _____

5. They wanted to help <u>America</u> win the war.   _____

6. Some workers helped build <u>airplanes</u>.   _____

7. Other women helped build <u>ships</u>.   _____

8. The American <u>soldiers</u> were thankful for their work.   _____

9. The <u>workers</u> were proud to help their country.   _____

10. They proved that women can do any <u>job</u>.   _____

American women helped
build ships and airplanes.

The 1940s: What We Did

A verb changes to show when an action happens.

Use a present tense verb to tell what happens now.

Today kids **listen** to CDs.

Use a past tense verb to tell what happened in the past. To form the past tense, you usually add -*ed*.

In the 1940s, kids **listened** to records.

Study the verbs in the box. They have a special form to show the past tense.

Present	Past
leave	left
are	were
say	said

Complete each sentence. Use the correct form of the verb from the box above.

Present

1.

Today families ___say___, "Let's watch TV."

Past

In the 1940s, they often _____, "Let's listen to the radio."

2.

Today a worker _____ milk at the store.

In the 1940s, a worker _____ milk at someone's house.

3.

Now CDs _____ popular.

In the 1940s, records _____ popular.

Name _____   Date _____

I Flew with Them

When you use a pronoun, be sure to tell about the right person.

Use these pronouns after an action verb and after words like *to*, *in*, or *with*.

Pronoun	Use:	Example
me	for yourself	She showed the pictures to **me**.
you	to talk to another person or persons	I will look at them with **you**.
us	for yourself and another person	She told **us** about the women pilots in World War II.
him, her, it, or **them**	to tell about other people or things	She flew with **them**.

Complete each sentence. Write the correct pronoun.

1.

This is a photo of ____me____ when I was a
(me / you)

pilot. This is Ann. I still write to _____ .
(him / her)

I will tell _____ what we did during
(me / you)
World War II.

2.

There were hundreds of _____ in our
(you / us)

group. We worked with male pilots. We helped

_____ practice. Factories built new
(them / us)

planes. We tested _____ .
(them / it)

© Hampton-Brown

WRITING PROJECT: COMPARISON POSTER

Then and Now

**Make a comparison poster for your class. Use your chart
to compare life in the 1940s with your life today.**

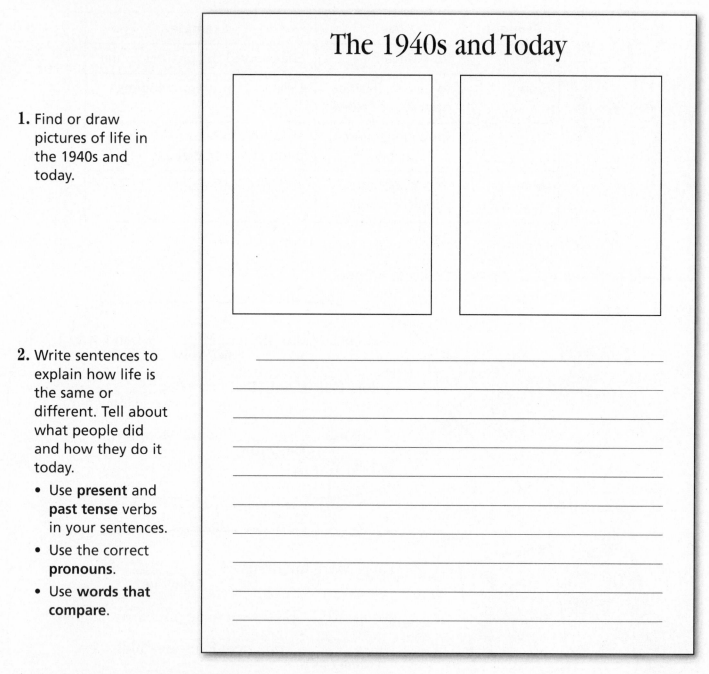

1. Find or draw
pictures of life in
the 1940s and
today.

The 1940s and Today

2. Write sentences to
explain how life is
the same or
different. Tell about
what people did
and how they do it
today.

• Use **present** and
past tense verbs
in your sentences.

• Use the correct
pronouns.

• Use **words that
compare**.

Put your work on a poster.

Read your poster to the class.

What Should the Characters Do?

Study the picture. Complete the chart.

What's in a Story?

A **character** is a person or animal in a story.

The **setting** is the time and place that the story happens.

The **plot** is what happens in the story from the **beginning** to the **middle** to the **end**.

Story Elements

Characters		
superhero shark monster swimmer	the ocean early in the morning	A man swims in the ocean. A monster chases him. A shark comes. A superhero saves the man.

Write about the story. What should the characters do?
Give them advice. Use the chart.

1. **Superhero:** _____

2. **Shark:** _____

3. **Swimmer:** _____

© Hampton-Brown

Two Sides of the Story

Name each character. Use words from the box.

tall giant	good fairy	old woman
brave girl	short elf	strong bear

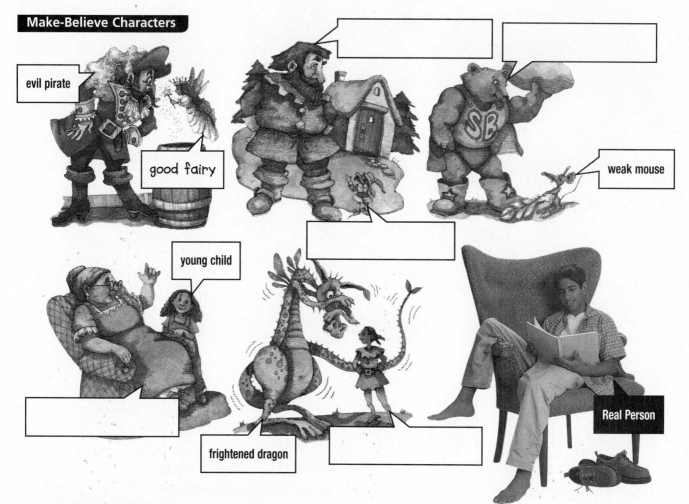

Make-Believe Characters

evil pirate

good fairy

weak mouse

young child

frightened dragon

Real Person

ASK FOR AND ACCEPT A FAVOR

The young child asks the old woman for a favor. Complete their sentences.

1. **Young Child:** Can you _____ ?

   Old Woman: Yes, I _____ .

2. **Old Woman:** I will _____ .

   Young Child: _____ ! You are very nice!

© Hampton-Brown

VOCABULARY: PHRASES FOR TIMES AND PLACES

A Time and a Place for Everything

Complete each sentence. Use words from the box.

From 6:00 to 7:00 a.m.	up the mountain
At night	across the river

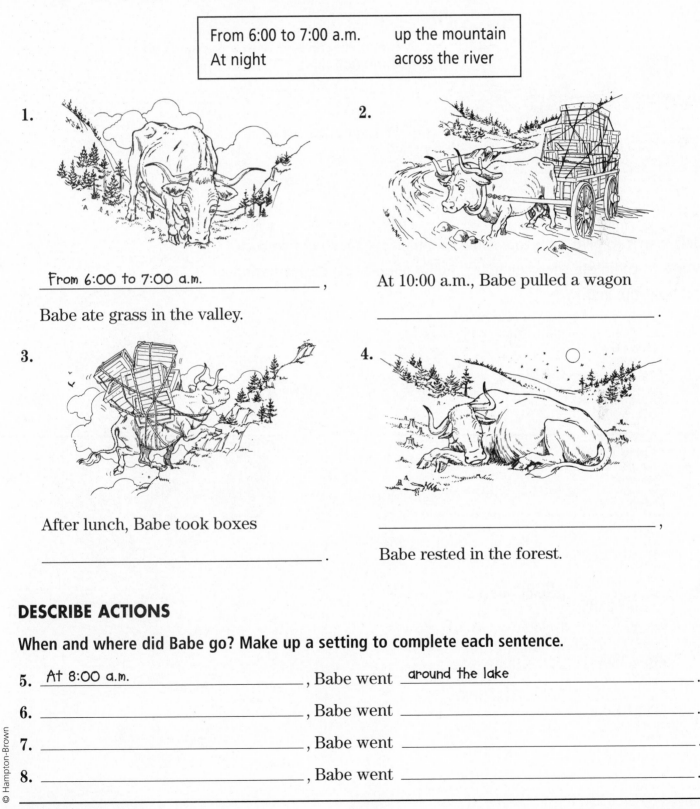

1.

_From 6:00 to 7:00 a.m._____ ,

Babe ate grass in the valley.

2.

At 10:00 a.m., Babe pulled a wagon

_____ .

3.

After lunch, Babe took boxes

_____ .

4.

_____ ,

Babe rested in the forest.

DESCRIBE ACTIONS

When and where did Babe go? Make up a setting to complete each sentence.

5. _At 8:00 a.m._____ , Babe went _around the lake_____ .

6. _____ , Babe went _____ .

7. _____ , Babe went _____ .

8. _____ , Babe went _____ .

COMMANDS

A Genie at His Command

A command tells someone to do something.

A command can end with a period or an exclamation mark.

> Listen to my command.
> Go outside.
> Put the trash away!

Jeff wants to give the genie some commands. Choose the correct word to complete each command. Add a period or an exclamation mark at the end.

1. _____Get_____ bikes for my friends _!_
   (Get / Go)

2. _____ me a box of jewels __
   (Bring / Grow)

3. _____ some music for me __
   (Play / Paint)

4. _____ new sneakers on my feet __
   (Sing / Put)

5. _____ a big house for my mother __
   (Plant / Build)

6. _____ me a story __
   (Take / Tell)

7. _____ a sandwich for me __
   (Do / Make)

8. _____ me to the mall __
   (Put / Take)

© Hampton-Brown

WRITING PROJECT: NEW STORY ENDING

Be a Storyteller

Write a new ending for *The Eagle and the Moon Gold*.

Make a storyboard to plan your ending. Follow these steps.

1. Think about your story idea.

2. Then draw a picture of each event.

3. Write a sentence under each picture. Tell what the **characters** do.
Use **time words** to show when things happen.

Event 1	Event 2
Sentence 1	**Sentence 2**

Event 3	Event 4
Sentence 3	**Sentence 4**

Put your storyboard on heavy paper.

Use the ideas on your storyboard to make up a new story ending.

Tell your story ending to the class.

Name _____ Date _____

About the Body

Read the question. Complete the answer. Use words from the chart.

The Body

skeleton	stomach
heart	nerves
lungs	brain
muscles	

What Body Parts Do			
help you move	helps you stand	digests food	breathe air
sense feelings	pumps blood	tells your body how to act	

1.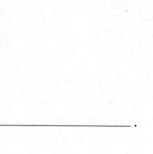

What do nerves do?

They ___sense feelings_____ .

2.

What does the brain do?

It _____ .

3.

What do muscles do?

They _____ .

4.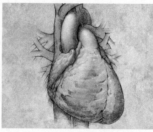

What does the heart do?

It _____ .

5.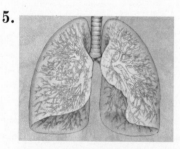

What do the lungs do?

They _____ .

6.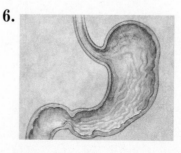

What does the stomach do?

It _____ .

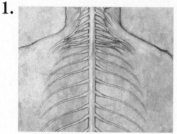

© Hampton-Brown

PRESENT TENSE VERBS

Our Workout Routine

Use present tense verbs to tell what happens all the time.

Each morning we **meet** at the pool.

We always **swim** one mile.

We **stretch** before every swim.

Every day we **exercise** together.

Complete each sentence. Use verbs from the box.

cheer	play	race	ride	wear	go

1. We _____race_____ every week.

2. People always _____ for us.

3. Each Saturday the girls _____ soccer.

4. They _____ their uniforms during every game.

5. Every day I _____ in the park.

6. I always _____ as fast as I can.

© Hampton-Brown

Meet the Athletes

Look at each picture and read the sentence below it. Name what you see.
Use words from the box.

scoreboard	hoop	racket	tennis ball
trophy	net	fans	coach

scoreboard

They play basketball.

Wendy plays tennis with her friends.

EXPRESS THANKS

Your team just won a trophy for one of the games above.
Write a thank-you speech. Thank your coach and the fans.

Thank you _____ for _____ .

We want to _____ .

Our coach _____ .

We also _____ .

_____ .

Watch Us Play

Use the correct pronoun when you talk about a person, place, or thing.

Use these pronouns to tell who does the action.

I	you	he	she	it	we	they

He took the ball.

Use these pronouns after an action verb or after a word like *to*, *for*, or *with*.

me	you	him	her	it	us	them

He ran with **it**.   They chased **him**.

Complete each sentence. Add the correct pronoun.

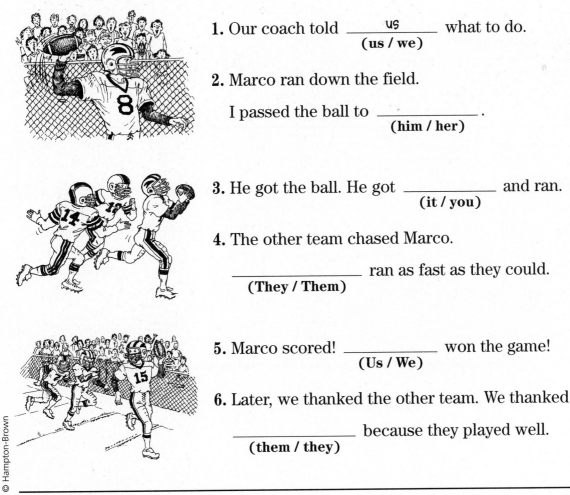

1. Our coach told ____us____ what to do.
   (us / we)

2. Marco ran down the field.

   I passed the ball to _____ .
   (him / her)

3. He got the ball. He got _____ and ran.
   (it / you)

4. The other team chased Marco.

   _____ ran as fast as they could.
   (They / Them)

5. Marco scored! _____ won the game!
   (Us / We)

6. Later, we thanked the other team. We thanked

   _____ because they played well.
   (them / they)

WRITING PROJECT: CLASS BOOK ON HEALTHY HABITS

In Top Shape

Choose a healthy habit to write about. Make a main idea diagram to show your ideas. Then write a paragraph for a class book. Follow these steps.

1. Find or draw a picture about your topic.

2. Look at your main idea diagram. Write the topic sentence. It tells the **main idea**.

3. Add three **details**. They tell more about the main idea.

4. Read your paragraph. Make sure each sentence tells about the main idea.

Type your paragraph or copy it onto a clean sheet of paper.

Add a picture. Then put your page in the class "Healthy Habits" book.

VOCABULARY: AMERICAN HISTORY

Who Built America?

Write a question for each answer. Use questions from the box.

People in History

Pilgrims
colonists
explorers
pioneers
immigrants

Who sent them there?	What did they build?
Where did they land?	Where did they explore?
When did their trip start?	When did they cross the sea?
Who sailed to America?	What did they study?

The Pilgrims sailed from England to America.

Lewis and Clark explored the West for President Jefferson.

1. Who sailed to America? _____

The Pilgrims sailed to America.

2. _____

They crossed the sea in 1620.

3. _____

They landed in Plymouth.

4. _____

They built a colony.

5. _____

They explored the West.

6. _____

President Thomas Jefferson sent them.

7. _____

Their trip started in 1804.

8. _____

They studied the land and animals.

People of America

You can use the word *how* or *why* to ask a question.

Use *how* to ask about the way people do something.

How did some explorers travel?

Some explorers traveled on horseback.

Use *why* to ask for a reason.

Why did they ride horses?

They rode horses **because** horses moved well and fast on rough land.

> You can use *because* to answer a question with *why*.

Read each answer. Then write two questions to go with the answer.

Pioneers traveled slowly because their wagons were full and heavy.

1. How   _did pioneers travel_____ ?

2. Why   _____ ?

Pioneers used wood to build their homes because there were a lot of trees.

3. How   _____ ?

4. Why   _____ ?

Some explorers traveled in boats because it was the easiest way to travel.

5. How   _____ ?

6. Why   _____ ?

Name _____ Date _____

Our Natural Treasures

Look at the map. Name each landform or body of water. Use words from the box.

| mountain | plains | ocean | river | lake |

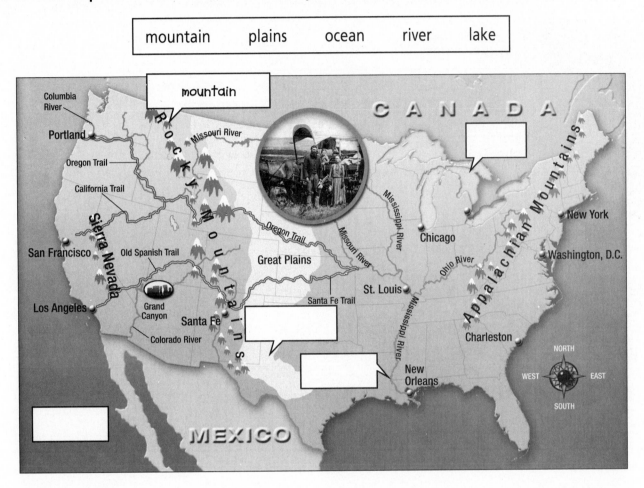

GIVE DIRECTIONS

Read each sentence. Use the map to give directions.

1. Tell the pioneers how to go from Los Angeles to Santa Fe.

Go east on the ___Old Spanish Trail___ . Cross the _____ .

Keep going _____ to Santa Fe.

2. Tell the pioneers how to go from New Orleans to Portland.

Go north along _____ to St. Louis. Go west on the

_____ . Cross the _____ . Keep going

_____ to Portland.

© Hampton-Brown

CAPITALIZATION: PROPER NOUNS

An American Explorer

A proper noun names a particular person, place, or thing.

John Muir

Capitalize the proper names of:	Examples
countries, cities, and states	John Muir walked across **America**. He walked from **Indianapolis**, **Indiana**, to **Cedar Key**, **Florida**.
bodies of water	Muir explored **Glacier Bay**, Alaska.
landforms	**Muir Glacier** was named after John Muir.

Write each sentence again. Capitalize the proper nouns.

1. John Muir was born in dunbar, scotland, in 1838.

John Muir was born in Dunbar, Scotland, in 1838.

2. Later he moved to portage, wisconsin, near beautiful fountain lake.

_____

3. Muir walked from indiana to the gulf of mexico.

_____

4. He studied plants and animals in yosemite valley, by the sierra mountains of california.

_____

5. Muir explored parts of canada and alaska.

_____

6. He studied forests in russia, india, and other countries.

_____

WRITING PROJECT: BIOGRAPHICAL SKETCH

A Famous American

Write a paragraph about a famous American. Use your notes
to tell what makes the person special. Follow these steps.

1. Write a title.

2. Write a **topic sentence.**
   Tell the person's name
   and what he or she did.

3. Add the **details.**
   • Tell **when** and **where**
     the person lived.
   • Tell **why** the person
     is famous.
   • Tell **how** the person
     helped the United
     States.

Type or copy your paragraph on a clean sheet of paper.

Add illustrations, if you like.

Read your paragraph to the class.

The Market Price

Study the word boxes.

Questions
How many oranges are in a bag?
How much is one bunch of grapes?
How many peppers can I buy for $1.00?
How much do the carrots cost?

Answers
You can buy 3 peppers.
There are twelve in a bag.
The carrots are 50¢ a pound.
A bunch of grapes costs $1.00.

Questions

Use *how many* to ask about things you can count.

How many carrots are in a pound?

How many apples can I buy for $3.00?

Use *how much* to ask about a price.

How much do the peppers cost?

How much are the tomatoes?

What do the people say? Write questions and answers from the boxes.

1.

How much do the carrots cost?

2.

There are twelve in a bag.

© Hampton-Brown

VOCABULARY: FARMING

Down on the Farm

Name what you see in each picture. Use words from the box.

rows	crop	seedlings	farmer	tractor	soil	crate

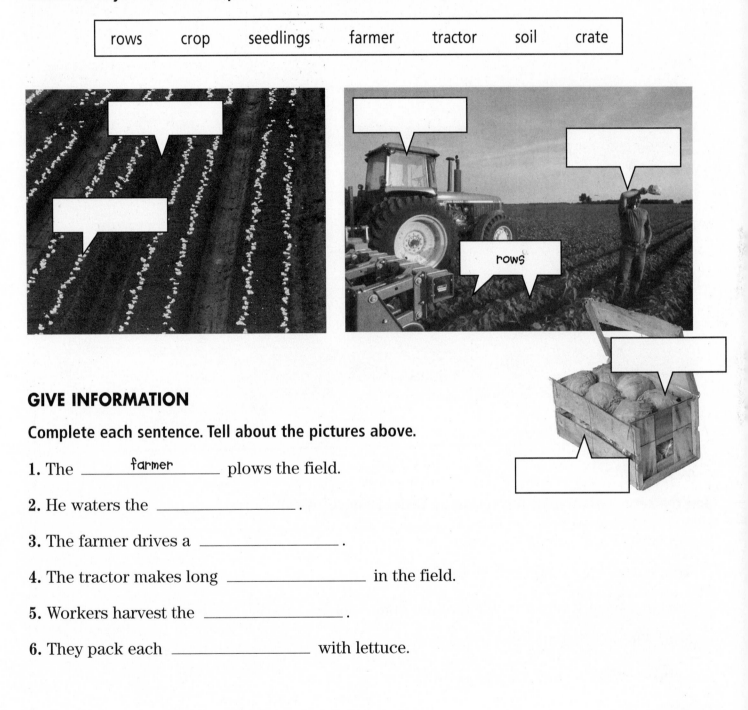

rows

GIVE INFORMATION

Complete each sentence. Tell about the pictures above.

1. The _____farmer_____ plows the field.

2. He waters the _____.

3. The farmer drives a _____.

4. The tractor makes long _____ in the field.

5. Workers harvest the _____.

6. They pack each _____ with lettuce.

Place Your Order

Name what you see in the picture. Use words from the box.

customer	place setting	server	check

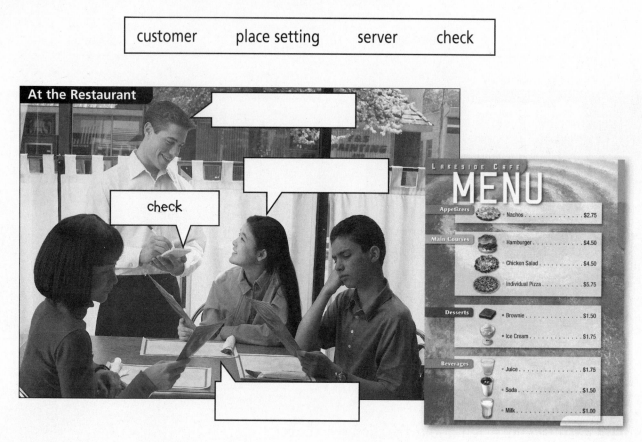

ORDER ITEMS

Tell the server what you want for lunch. Order from the menu above.

1. Server: Would you like an appetizer?

    You: Yes. I want <u>some nachos, please</u>.

2. Server: What would you like for your main course?

    You: Please bring me _____.

3. Server: What would you like to drink?

    You: I _____.

4. Server: Would you like a dessert?

    You: Yes. I _____.

SENSORY ADJECTIVES

Describe the Food

An adjective can tell how something looks, feels, smells, sounds, or tastes.

This apple smells **fresh**. It is **smooth** and **shiny**. It sounds **crisp**. This apple tastes **sweet** and **delicious**!

Describe the food in each picture. Choose adjectives from the box.

delicious	sweet	tangy	crunchy	loud	sticky
juicy	fresh	cold	warm	spicy	crisp

1.

The macaroni and cheese is
_____warm_____ and _____ .

2.

The taco sounds _____ and
_____ . It tastes _____ .

3.

The ice cream tastes _____ . It
is _____ and _____ .

4.

The orange smells _____ . It is
_____ and _____ .

WRITING PROJECT: CROP REPORT

Comparing Crops

Write a crop report for your class. Use a Venn diagram
to compare two crops. Then follow these steps.

1. Write a title. Name
the two crops you
want to compare.

2. Write a topic
sentence. Name the
two crops again.

3. Turn the ideas in
your Venn diagram
into sentences.

• Tell how the crops
are **alike**. Use
the words *both*
and *and*.

• Tell how the crops
are **different**. Use
the word *but*.

• Tell how the crops
look and taste. Use
sensory adjectives
like *small*, *red*, or
sour. Get more
ideas from pages
310–311 of your
Handbook.

Crop Report:

_____ and _____

Copy your report or type it on a computer.

You may want to add pictures.

Read your report to the class.

© Hampton-Brown

Do You Agree?

What can you say to agree or disagree? Study the chart.

I Agree	I Disagree
You are right.	No way!
That is so true!	You are wrong.
I think so, too.	That isn't true.
You bet!	I don't think so.

Idioms

No way!
no good
one of a kind
leave all other
  bands behind

Read each opinion. Do you agree or disagree? Write your opinion.
Use some of the words in the chart.

1.

Rock bands play the best music.

That is so true! Rock bands leave all

other bands behind!

_____

2.
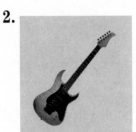
The guitar is the most important part of a rock band.

_____

_____

3.

Most kids like to dance to music.

_____

_____

4.

Country music stars sing better than rock stars.

_____

_____

FUTURE TENSE VERBS AND CONTRACTIONS

You Will Be a Star!

A verb in the future tense tells what will happen later, or in the future.

Here are some ways to show the future tense.

will + verb	Our band **will play** new songs next week.
am are + going to + verb is	**I am going to sing.** You **are going to play** the drums. The concert **is going to be** great!
we'll + verb	We will write new music. **We'll write** new music. The contraction for *we will* is *we'll*.
won't + verb	We will not play our old songs. We **won't play** our old songs. The contraction for *will not* is *won't*.

Complete each sentence. Tell about the future. Use words from the box.

1. Miguel _____is going to join_____ a jazz band.

2. He _____ rock music.

3. Sally _____ a singer.

4. She _____ the words to the song.

5. The boys _____ music.

6. They _____ someone to play it.

will find is going to join won't forget will write won't play is going to be

© Hampton-Brown

Outer Space

Name what you see in each picture. Use words from the box.

| galaxy | shooting star | star | Moon | Sun | planets |

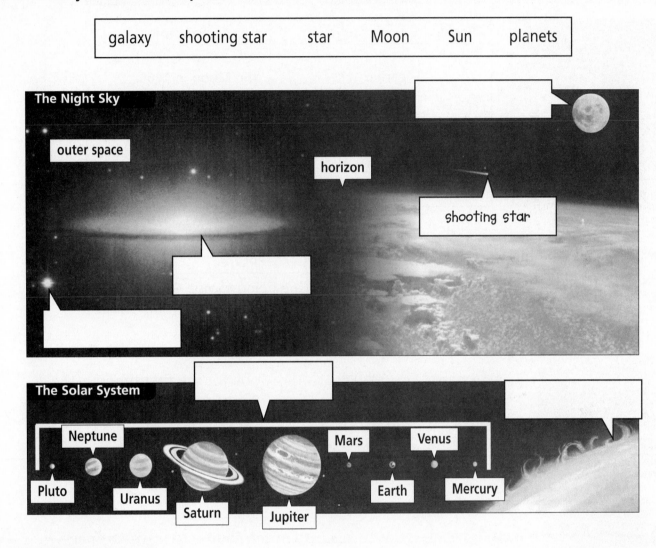

GIVE INFORMATION

Complete each sentence. Write facts about the night sky and the solar system.

1. _____Mars_____ is the fourth planet from the Sun.

2. There are nine _____ in our solar system.

3. The name of our planet is _____ .

4. _____ is the biggest planet.

5. The night sky has billions of _____ .

VERB TENSES

They Went to the Moon

The tense of a verb shows when the action happens.

Tense	Tells	Example
Past	what happened earlier	Astronauts **landed** on the Moon in 1969.
Present	what is happening now	Astronauts still **explore** space.
Future	what will happen later	Some day they **will visit** Mars. They **are going to do** experiments there.

Complete each sentence. Use words from the chart.

Past	Present	Future
visited	visits	are going to visit
used	use	will use

1. Astronauts _____*visited*_____ the Moon for the first time on July 20, 1969.

2. On that day, they _____ a space ship called a lunar module.

3. Today they _____ a space shuttle to travel in space.

4. It _____ a space station.

5. In the future, they _____ Mars.

6. Astronauts _____ new machines to explore Mars.

© Hampton-Brown

VERB TENSES

The Moon Glows

The tense of a verb shows when the action happens.

Tense	Tells	Example
Past	what happened earlier	Last week, the Moon **was** full.
Present	what is happening now	Tonight I **see** part of the Moon.
Future	what will happen later	In three weeks, the Moon **will be** full again. The sky **is going to be** very bright.

Complete each sentence. Write the correct form of the verb.

1. Every night, Dana _____likes_____ to look at the sky.
   (like)

2. Sometimes she can't _____ the Moon.
   (see)

3. Two weeks ago, there _____ no Moon.
   (is)

4. Last night, clouds _____ it.
   (cover)

5. Tomorrow Dana _____ to see the Moon.
   (try)

6. She hopes it _____ in the sky.
   (glow)

7. Dana is going to _____ more about the Moon and stars.
   (learn)

8. She is going to _____ a picture of the night sky.
   (draw)

WRITING PROJECT: DIAMANTE POEM

Star Poetry

Write a poem about two things in outer space.
Follow these steps.

1. At the top, write a **noun** that names one thing in outer space. Write a different noun at the bottom.

2. Write 2 **adjectives** that describe the noun at the top.

3. Write 3 **verbs** that end in **-ing**. The verbs should tell about both nouns.

4. Write 2 **adjectives** that describe the noun at the bottom.

5. Make a star shape. Copy your poem on one side. Write facts about the 2 things in outer space on the other side.

_____ noun

_____ _____ adjectives

_____ verbs with **-ing** _____

_____ _____ adjectives

_____ noun

Decorate your star.

Read your poem and facts to the class.

© Hampton-Brown